The Complete Guide to Veterans' Benefits

Bruce C. Brown

THE COMPLETE GUIDE TO VETERANS' BENEFITS: EVERYTHING YOU NEED TO KNOW EXPLAINED SIMPLY

Copyright © 2014 Atlantic Publishing Group, Inc.
1405 SW 6th Avenue • Ocala, Florida 34471 • Phone 800-814-1132 • Fax 352-622-1875
Website: www.atlantic-pub.com • E-mail: sales@atlantic-pub.com
SAN Number: 268-1250

Library of Congress Cataloging-in-Publication Data

Brown, Bruce C. (Bruce Cameron), 1965-
The complete guide to veterans' benefits : everything you need to know explained simply / by Bruce C. Brown.
p. cm.
Includes bibliographical references and index.
ISBN 978-1-60138-702-8 (alk. paper) -- ISBN 1-60138-702-4 (alk. paper) 1. Veterans--Services for--United States. 2. Military pensions--United States. I. Title.
UB357.B75 2012
362.860973--dc23
2012001511

INTERIOR LAYOUT: Antoinette D'Amore • addesign@videotron.ca
COVER DESIGN: Jacqueline Miller • millerjackiej@gmail.com

Printed on Recycled Paper

Reduce. Reuse.
RECYCLE.

A decade ago, Atlantic Publishing signed the Green Press Initiative. These guidelines promote environmentally friendly practices, such as using recycled stock and vegetable-based inks, avoiding waste, choosing energy-efficient resources, and promoting a no-pulping policy. We now use 100-percent recycled stock on all our books. The results: in one year, switching to post-consumer recycled stock saved 24 mature trees, 5,000 gallons of water, the equivalent of the total energy used for one home in a year, and the equivalent of the greenhouse gases from one car driven for a year.

Over the years, we have adopted a number of dogs from rescues and shelters. First there was Bear and after he passed, Ginger and Scout. Now, we have Kira, another rescue. They have brought immense joy and love not just into our lives, but into the lives of all who met them.

We want you to know a portion of the profits of this book will be donated in Bear, Ginger and Scout's memory to local animal shelters, parks, conservation organizations, and other individuals and nonprofit organizations in need of assistance.

– Douglas & Sherri Brown,
President & Vice-President of Atlantic Publishing

Disclaimer

The material in this book is provided for informational purposes and as a general guide to the benefits offered to veterans. Basic definitions of laws are provided according to the status of the laws at the time of printing; be sure to check for a change or update in laws and eligibility. This book should not substitute VA or other military counsel for the use and application of veterans' benefits.

Dedication

This book is dedicated to Coast Guard UF-2G Albatross #1240 (Grumman HU-16E), which was lost on March 5, 1967. On a Sunday night search and rescue case, the aircraft and crew responded to a vessel reportedly taking on water 20 miles off the Florida coast. The entire crew perished when their seaplane struck the water. The captain of the fishing vessel reported seeing an orange glow two miles southeast of his position. The crash occurred approximately 22 miles east of Apalachicola. A fleet of U.S. Coast Guard and Navy vessels and aircraft combed the area. The wreck of the UF-2G Albatross #1240 was not found for nearly 40 years. In July 2006, A.U.E. divers investigated the wreck of an unidentified aircraft resting offshore Carrabelle. The site was dominated by the aircraft's wing and two radial engines. Both engines had become dislodged from their mounts, though no trace of their propellers was observed. The nose was heavily damaged, and the cockpit was all but absent. The lower hull of the fuselage was largely collapsed, which complicated the initial identification as an amphibious aircraft. The aft portion of the fuselage was fractured, with the tail resting parallel to the wing and on its starboard side. Based on the diagnostic features observed on the wreckage, the location of the site in relation to the historical account of the crash, the lack of other documented aviation accidents in the general area, and expert opinions, the wreck was identified as U.S. Coast Guard UF-2G Albatross #1240.

Source: http://uwex.us/uscg1240.htm, www.zianet.com/tmorris/saintpete.html

"The willingness with which our young people are likely to serve in any war, no matter how justified, is directly proportional to how they perceive the veterans of earlier wars were treated and appreciated."

— George Washington, president of the United States

"We often take for granted the very things that most deserve our gratitude."

— Cynthia Ozick, American novelist

"This nation will remain the land of the free only so long as it is the home of the brave."

— Elmer Davis, director, United States Office of War Information

Table of Contents

Chapter 5: TRICARE Health Care Program 105

Chapter 8: Life Insurance Benefits During and After your Military Career 165

Chapter 9: Veterans Home Loan Program............ 179

Chapter 10: Veteran Scholarships, Grants, and Aid... 191

Introduction

According to the U.S. Census Bureau and the American Veterans By the Numbers website from Infoplease® at (**www.infoplease.com/spot/veteranscensus1.html#ixzz1ZWqJWv9e**), as of 2012, there were approximately 21.2 million veterans in the United States. More than 837,000 of the veterans in our country served in both Gulf War eras. More than 211,000 served during both the Korean War and the Vietnam era, and 147,000 served during both World War II and the Korean War. And 54,000 remaining veterans served during World War II, the Korean War, *and* the Vietnam era. More than two million U.S. servicemen and women have served tours of duty in Afghanistan and Iraq.

When not on active duty, more than 20 percent of vets do not have health care coverage, and many more are unaware of the hundreds of benefits to which they have access. As a result, many are suffering financial strain during and after deployment. And there were 9.6 million veterans aged 65 and older in 2012. This is a discouraging statistic because federal and state governments, as well as private foundations, have numerous scholarships and military discounts available only to veterans. There are billions of dollars in aid available, waiting to be claimed, but the problem is finding and properly applying for these programs.

As a veteran of the United States Armed Forces, I was eager to write a book that could educate the millions of former, current, and future veterans on what benefits they are entitled to as a result of their military service to our great nation. The key word is entitled. Veterans serve their country and in return are granted entitlements under United States law. This book sets the record straight on what those entitlements are, explains how to maximize veterans' benefits, and opens the door to a wealth of veterans' benefits information in a single source, rather than leaving the veteran to navigate myriad disconnected systems, websites, and information sources available. Our armed forces have a good program for transitioning active duty and reserve military members to retirement. However, the transitional benefit programs for those who are discharged, released from active duty, or medically disabled, and those who choose to leave the military after their service commitment are often less than adequate.

This is the 13th book I have written for publication, and unlike my previous books, this one is not related to online marketing, the Internet, search engines, blogging, building websites, email marketing, or how to succeed with establishing an online business. I am a military veteran with just under 28 years of active duty service in the U.S. Coast Guard and have advanced from seaman apprentice to commander. I had an approved retirement for the spring of 2008, and I was just beginning the transition process from military to civilian life, but a last-minute job offer from the Coast Guard for a position in Miami was presented to me, and I opted to "extend" my military career a few more years. But I know how stressful a time retirement or discharge is for most career military persons because they are leaving the comfort zone they have known for the better part of their lives and are entering "unknown" often unstable and always-competitive civilian workforce environment. The economy today is in turmoil with record unemployment and uncertain job markets, so your veterans' benefits are even more valuable than ever before.

Korean War Veterans' Memorial in Washington, D.C.

I hope this book serves every veteran as a resource guide to help him or her navigate the veterans' benefits programs, maximize the benefits which he or she receives, and achieve success in a post-military career. My sincere desire is that this finds its way into each veteran's backpack, onto his or her desk, and into his or her home and becomes a comprehensive resource to use often.

Who Is this Book For?

As a veteran, you are entitled to a multitude of benefits and preferences. It is your right to claim these benefits, and this book will help you to do exactly that. This book provides candid, no-nonsense advice and practical information you can use to maximize your benefits while simplifying the often-confusing bureaucratic veterans' benefits system. Your primary partners for veterans' benefits will be the Veterans Benefits Association, the Veterans Health Care Administration, and the Department of Veterans Affairs (VA).

The mission of the Veterans Benefits Administration (VBA), in partnership with the Veterans Health Administration (VHA) and the National Cemetery Administration (NCA), is to provide benefits and services to the veterans and their families in a responsive, timely, and compassionate manner in recognition of their service to the nation. The Veterans Benefit Administration is part of the VA.

The Board of Veterans' Appeals (also known as "BVA" or "the Board") is also part of the VA, located in Washington, D.C. Members of the board review claim determinations made by local VA offices and issue decisions on appeals. These law judges, attorneys experienced in veterans law and in reviewing benefit claims, are the only ones who can issue board decisions. Staff attorneys, also trained in veterans law, review the facts of each appeal and assist the board members.

Anyone who is not satisfied with the results of a claim for veterans' benefits (determined by a VA regional office, medical center, or other local VA office) should read the "How do I Appeal" pamphlet available for free download at **http://www.bva.va.gov/docs/Pamphlets/010202A.pdf**. It is intended to explain the steps involved in filing an appeal and to serve as a reference for the terms and abbreviations used in the appeal process. Your next step is to file a Notice of Disagreement and Statement of the Case, both of which are described in the pamphlet mentioned.

This book covers all aspects of military benefits program, including the Post-9/11 GI Bill and the most recent changes that went into effect in 2011. It is an ideal companion for any active duty, reserve, and guard members who are leaving the military in the future, have recently left the military, are preparing for retirement, or are under a medical discharge or medical retirement. It is also a handy resource for the spouses and dependents of veterans, as it contains several chapters about survivor benefits and benefits for the family of veterans. The book discusses veterans' benefits for Vietnam, Korean, WWII, and other era veterans; however, it is geared predominately for modern-day veterans.

This book is broken down by various chapters, each covering critical information about your veterans' benefits programs and entitlements. You do not need to read this book in any particular order, simply navigate to the chapter relevant to your situation or topic. Good luck, and thank you for your service.

Chapter 1

Who is a Veteran?

Many Americans still do not understand what or who a veteran is. Often, they believe a veteran is someone who has been severely wounded or killed in battle. However, a veteran, as defined by U.S. federal law, is any person who has served for any length of time in any branch of the United States Armed Forces. The uniformed services include:

- U.S. Army
- U.S. Air Force
- U.S. Navy
- U.S. Marine Corps
- U.S. Coast Guard
- Commissioned Corps of the Public Health Service
- Commissioned Corps of the National Oceanic and Atmospheric Association

A war veteran is any person, serving in any branch of the USAF, who was ordered to foreign soil or waters to participate in direct or non-direct support activity against any enemy of the United States. A combat veteran is any person, serving in any branch of the military, who experiences any level of hostility or engages in enemy combatant action for any duration of time resulting from offensive, defensive, or friendly fire military action involving a real or perceived enemy in a pre- or post-designated combat operations. Reservists and members who have served in the National Guard or the Air National Guard are also veterans and have certain benefits and entitlements, depending on length of service and locality of service (in particular if they served in an active duty combat status).

A common myth is that a veteran is not a veteran until he or she retires from the military. Although it is true that military retirees are veterans, they became veterans when they first enter the military (in most cases). Military retirees are veterans; however, many other current active duty, reserve, and guard members are veterans. Even more who served their country for a

specified period under their contract that have been discharged under honorable or general conditions are also veterans.

Although this qualification is typically simple in the case of career military or military retirees, it become extremely complicated for single-term enlistees, reservists, and guard members. As you will discover, there are different "types" of veterans, and depending on your veteran status, you have different type of veterans' benefits and entitlements. In some cases, you might have no benefits or entitlements at all. There is no "cookie-cutter" definition for a veteran that translates easily into veterans' benefits. Keep in mind, when dealing with the Department of Veterans Affairs (VA), the burden falls on you to prove your veteran status.

Keeping your discharge papers, DD-214, copies of your service and health records, and other important personnel paperwork is critical to obtaining veterans' benefits efficiently, and a great deal of patience is necessary. The "red tape" is often long and frustrating. Patience, in this case, is a virtue, as it may take weeks or months for any significant action to be taken on your claim package, depending on what benefits you are trying to take advantage of. In defense of the VA, many benefits are easy to obtain and are given routinely in an expeditious and relatively simple manner.

Many benefits have been around for years, and the eligibility requirements are clear and simple to understand. Others are much more complicated and can change based on congressional regulations determined by honorable discharge or under honorable conditions status. They also can change based on the law as enacted through the legislative process or based on specific type or location of service (i.e. Afghanistan, Iraq, Vietnam), which can qualify you for certain benefits only if you served in designated combat regions. This is particularly true for reserve and guard veterans.

Types of Veterans

If you have served in the U.S. military and have been discharged under honorable or general conditions, are retired, or are medically discharged, you are a veteran. The majority of veterans are those who served for a period of service and were honorable discharged upon the completion of their service commitment. It is important to note that most veterans fall into either this category or the retired military category. However, when you served, for how long, what combat operations you participated in, and what your discharge status was all factored into what veterans' benefits you might be eligible for and entitled to. Here is a list of some of the types of veterans, which will help you decide what benefits you could successfully claim:

- **Honorable or general discharged veteran:** A person who has served in the USAF for any period, is not entitled to retirement benefits, and was discharged under general or honorable conditions is entitled to certain benefits through the VA. Certain entitlements and benefits are based upon length of service and type of service, such as combat-related duties. In general, discharges characterized as other than honorable, or bad conduct discharges, offer limited to no veterans' benefits.

- **Military retiree:** A person who has served in the USAF for more than 20 years and is eligible for a full military retirement package. Some services, such as the U.S. Coast Guard, offered early military retirement packages under the Clinton era as an incentive to reduce the overall size of the military. Those who took advantage of this early retirement also are entitled to military retirement pay and a comprehensive benefit package. This includes those on a medically retired status. Retirees are eligible for a wide array of benefits, entitlements, and privileges and access to military bases for exchange, commissary, and medical benefits. However, some benefits and entitlements may be limited by congressional regulation.

- **Disabled veteran:** A person who has served in the USAF and who has suffered wounds, physical ailments, medical conditions, or illness as a result of his or her military service. He or she is given a disability rating, which is labeled as a percentage. The higher the percentage, the more severe the disability and the more the veteran will be qualified for. Disabled veterans are entitled to a compensation package between 10 and 100 percent based on the severity of their condition and the most current compensation rate table, available at **www.vba.va.gov/bln/21/Rates/comp01.htm**. The actual condition does not necessarily have to have been combat related, such as medical complication from an improved explosive device. In other words, an off-duty sports injury while on active duty typically qualifies as service related. This is one of the most widely claimed veteran benefits because it qualifies you for financial and medical benefits. *Later chapters of this book will cover disability in depth.*

Combat veterans

Certain VA benefits require wartime service. Even if the veteran him or herself is no longer living, his or her dependents still might be eligible to receive certain compensations from the VA. Check this list to see if you or one of your parents would be considered a combat veteran. Under the law, VA recognizes these war periods:

Indian wars. January 1, 1817, through December 31, 1898, inclusive. Service must have been rendered with the United States military forces against Indian tribes or nations.

Spanish-American War. April 21, 1898, through July 4, 1902, inclusive. If the veteran served with the United States military forces engaged in hostilities in the Moro Province, the ending date is July 15, 1903. The Philippine Insurrection and the Boxer Rebellion are included.

Mexican border period. May 9, 1916, through April 5, 1917, in the case of a veteran who during such period served in Mexico, on the borders thereof, or in the waters adjacent thereto

World War I. April 6, 1917, through November 11, 1918, inclusive. If the veteran served with the United States military forces in Russia, the ending date is April 1, 1920. Service after November 11, 1918 and before July 2, 1921, is considered World War I service if the veteran served in the active military, naval, or air service after April 5, 1917, and before November 12, 1918.

World War II. December 7, 1941, through December 31, 1946, inclusive. If the veteran was in service on December 31, 1946, or in continuous service before July 26, 1947, this is considered World War II service.

Korean conflict. June 27, 1950, through January 31, 1955, inclusive

Vietnam era. The period beginning on February 28, 1961, and ending on May 7, 1975, inclusive, in the case of a veteran who served in the Republic of Vietnam during that period. The period beginning on August 5, 1964, and ending on May 7, 1975, inclusive, in all other cases (Authority: 38 U.S.C. 101(29))

Persian Gulf War. August 2, 1990, through date to be prescribed by presidential proclamation or law

Future dates. The period beginning on the date of any future declaration of war by the Congress and ending on a date prescribed by presidential proclamation or concurrent resolution of the Congress

Fiduciary Program

VA's Fiduciary Program is designed to protect the benefits paid to veterans and beneficiaries who are unable to manage their own financial affairs. To qualify for this service, a VA beneficiary must be either a minor or an adult who has been determined to be unable to manage his or her financial affairs by VA, or under legal disability because of court action. When VA benefits are payable to an individual who meets the above criteria, then a third party payee or fiduciary is appointed to ensure the beneficiary's funds are expended for the care, support, welfare, and needs of the beneficiary and their recognized dependents.

The Fiduciary Program's duty, mandated by Congress, is to provide oversight to fiduciaries by ensuring that they are providing the proper services for those beneficiaries who have shown a need of the program's protection. For more information, please visit the VA Fiduciary Program Web page at **www.vba. va.gov/bln/21/Fiduciary/index.htm**.

VA Benefits and Health Care Utilization

The VA produces some interesting statistics surrounding VA Benefits and Health Care Utilization that show how many veterans are benefiting from the various programs they offer and particular demographics based on use. This chart is produced by the Veterans Administration and was updated in 2013:

Updated 11/1/13

 VA Benefits & Health Care Utilization

Number of Veterans Receiving VA Disability Compensation (as of 09/30/13):	3.74 M
Number of Veterans Rated 100% Disabled (as of 09/30/13):	394,514
Number of Veterans Receiving VA Pension (as of 09/30/13):	303,261
Number of Spouses Receiving DIC (as of 09/30/13):	352,905
Number of Total Enrollees in VA Health Care System (FY 12):	8.76 M [1]
Number of Total Unique Patients Treated (FY 12):	6.33 M [1]
Number of Veterans Compensated for PTSD (as of 09/30/13):	625,953
Number of Veterans in Receipt of IU Benefits (as of 09/30/13):	317,854
Number of VA Education Beneficiaries (FY 12):	945,052
Number of Life Insurance Policies Supervised and Administered by VA (as of 09/30/13):	6.82 M
Face Amount of Insurance Policies Supervised and Administered by VA (as of 09/30/13):	1.31 T
Number of VA Voc Rehab (Chapter 31) Trainees (FY 13):	67,995
Number of Active VA Home Loan Participants (as of 06/30/13):	1.87 M
Number of Health Care Professionals Rotating Through VA (FY 12):	117,500
Number of OEF/OIF Amputees (as of 11/1/13):	1,634 [2]

Source: DVA Information Technology Center; Health Services Training Report; VBA Education Service; VBA Office of Performance Analysis & Integrity; [1] VHA (10A5); [2] DoD

Veterans Demographics

Projected U.S. Veterans Population:	21,973,000	{Female 2,271,000 10%}
Projected Number of Living WW II Veterans (as of 9/30/2013):		1,246,000
Estimated Number of WW II Veterans Pass Away Per Day:		413
Percentage of Veteran Population 65 or Older:		44.19%

Veteran Population by Race:
White 82.7%   Black 12.1%
Asian/Pacific Islander 1.4%   Other 3.0%
American Indian/Alaska Natives 0.8%   Hispanic 6.3%

About VA

Number of VA Employees in Pay Status:	336,920
Number of VA Hospitals:	151
Number of VA Community-Based Outpatient Clinics:	825
Number of VA Vet Centers:	300
Number of VBA Regional Offices:	56
Number of VA National Cemeteries:	131

FY11 Appropriations (actual)[1]		FY12 Appropriations (actual)[1]		FY13 Appropriations (enacted)[1]	
VA:	$126.6B[4]	VA:	$127B[4]	VA:	$137B[4]
VHA:	$51.5B[2]	VHA:	$54.2B[2]	VHA:	$56.3B[2]
VBA-GOE:	$2.13B[3]	VBA-GOE:	$2.04B[3]	VBA-GOE:	$2.16B[3]
NCA:	$249.5M	NCA:	$251M	NCA:	$258M
OIT:	$2.99B	OIT:	$3.10B	OIT:	$3.23B

Produced by the National Center for Veterans Analysis and Statistics
Source: Veteran Population as of 09/30/13; VA Employ Pay Status Count 09/30/13; Veterans Affairs Site Tracking (VAST) 06/30/13; NCA as of 09/30/13; Office of Budget; Health Services Training Report FY12 ; [1] Includes MCCF; [2] Medical Care w/ MCCF and medical research; [3] Discretionary Spending Only; [4] Includes funding from the Economic Recovery Act

Who is a Veteran?

You cannot tell a veteran just by looking, as the following poem from an unknown author illustrates. This poem is found on the Marine Corps website at **www.forcerecon.com/veteran.htm**.

Some veterans bear visible signs of their service: a missing limb, a jagged scar, a certain look in the eye.

Others carry the evidence inside them: a pin holding a bone together, a piece of shrapnel in the leg. Or perhaps another sort of steel — the soul's ally forged in the refinery of adversity.

Except in parades, however, the men and women who kept America safe wear no badge or emblem.

You can't tell a vet just by looking.

He is the cop on the beat who spent six months in Saudi Arabia sweating two gallons a day making sure armored personnel carriers didn't run out of fuel.

He is the barroom loudmouth, dumber than five wooden planks, whose overgrown frat-boy behavior is outweighed a hundred times in the cosmic scale by four hours of exquisite bravery near the 38th parallel.

She — or he — is the nurse who fought against futility and went to sleep sobbing every night for two solid years in Da Nang.

He is the POW who went away one person and came back another — or didn't come back AT ALL.

He is the Quantico drill instructor who has never seen combat — but has saved countless lives by turning slouchy, no-account rednecks and gang members into Marines, and teaching them to watch each other's backs.

He is the parade-riding Legionnaire who pins on his ribbons and medals with a prosthetic hand.

He is the career quartermaster who watched the ribbons and medals pass him by.

He is the three anonymous heroes in The Tomb of the Unknowns, whose presence at Arlington National Cemetery forever preserves the memory of all anonymous heroes whose valor died unrecognized on the battlefield or in the ocean's sunless deep.

He is the old guy bagging groceries at the supermarket — palsied and aggravatingly slow — who helped liberate a Nazi death camp, and who wishes all day long that his wife were still alive to hold him when the nightmares come.

He (or she) is an ordinary and yet an extraordinary, human being — a person who sacrificed his life's most vital years in the service of his country, and who sacrificed his ambitions so others would not have to sacrifice theirs.

He is a soldier and a savior and a sword against the darkness, and he is nothing more than the finest, greatest testimony on behalf of the finest, greatest nation ever known.

So remember, each time you see someone who has served our country, just lean over and say Thank you. That's all most people need, and in most cases it will mean more than any medals they could have been awarded or were awarded.

Two little words that mean a lot, "THANK YOU."

Remember that Nov. 11 is Veterans Day.

~Author Unknown

Wearing the military uniform and serving the people of the United States can be one of the most rewarding and enriching experiences of your life. By serving our nation, you are entitled to certain benefits, and this book will help you maximize those benefits. Remember, a veteran is a person who has served for any period in any branch of the United States Military Services. The length of service and type of discharge will determine what benefits you and your dependents are eligible for. No matter what you have survived or how you have benefited our country, you deserve all the information about what your country can now do for you.

Chapter 2

Preparing to Depart the Military

t some point in every military member's career, he or she must transition from military to civilian life. This typically is done one of the following ways: retirement, discharge/release from active duty (honorable, dishonorable, general, etc.), medical retirement, or medical discharge or disabled. Some component of reserves or guard members also transition from active duty back to their active or inactive reserve status. In all cases, these individuals are veterans. This chapter is written specifically for all military service members who are preparing to transition out of the military to civilian life in any of the above categories.

Departing the military, even with the peace of mind of having a retirement income to depend upon, is a stressful time for any veteran. Those who are departing due to disability or combat-related injury face the biggest challenge, as they not only have to deal with the physical and mental challenges associated with their disabilities, but also do not receive a military retirement pension (unless they were retirement eligible) and must navigate the murky and confusing halls of the Department of Veterans Affairs (VA) for support, benefits, and treatment.

Many military members have not held civilian jobs in years. Military skills do not transition easily to the civilian sector, and senior officers and enlisted military members might be junior to much younger individuals in the corporate environment. Even with military retirement, there is a definite drop in pay. Those who are leaving the military after serving their commitment will go from a steady paycheck to no paycheck at all. Luckily for all of those in uniform, each service has a wealth of programs designed to assist the military member with his or her transition.

Transition Assistance Program

All military branches have a transition program created under the VA. The Transition Assistance Program (TAP) helps departing military members prepare for and enter civilian life after their military service at less cost to both the military member and the government. TAP offers advice on finances, résumés, job search, and placement. It offers benefits for military members during their transition to civilian life, assistance, and related services.

The Departments of Defense, Veterans Affairs, Homeland Security, and the Department of Labor's Veterans' Employment and Training Service (VETS) support TAP. The TAP program is designed for military service members who are within 180 days of separation or retirement, as this program will help you transition from military service to civilian life.

The program takes places over one three- to five-day session, held at military installations nationwide. Attendees learn about how to perform a job search, complete a résumé, and dress for success. They discuss career decision-making, labor market conditions, and interview techniques. One of the most valuable things attendees receive is an honest appraisal of employability relative to the current job market and their skills, so they can set realistic expectations for future employment. Of course, veterans' benefits are covered in detail. Typically, each member is offered the opportunity to attend one TAP session before he or she separates or retires from the military.

VA's goal for TAP services is to ensure service members are aware of their VA benefits and to provide assistance as needed. For those leaving active duty due to medical problems, the outreach effort is intensified to ensure a full understanding of the VA compensation process and vocational rehabilitation and employment program.

Enrollment in a TAP class

It depends on the service you are in, but typically, TAP classes are announced routinely throughout the year and are easy to attend. Your Family Service Center, Command Career Counselors, Servicing Personnel Office, or other administrative support units should have application information and procedures readily available for you. Federal law requires a pre-separation counseling interview for all officer and enlisted members no later than 90 days before separation or retirement. At this interview, you will be given more information for TAP sessions taking place in your area.

For all anticipated retirements, pre-separation counseling will begin as soon as possible during the 24-month period preceding the anticipated retirement date. In the case of a separation other than a retirement, pre-separation counseling should begin as soon as possible during the 12-month period preceding the anticipated separation date. Ideally, the service member will attend the workshop no later than six to nine months before completion of the military obligation. Personnel should complete a TAP Workshop no later than 90 days before separation/retirement.

DOD has created a web portal for military transitioners at **www.turbotap. org/register.tpp**. This website features a brief overview of the DOD Transition Assistance Program, locations, and phone numbers of all transition assistance offices, and job search information and assistance. You also can find information, including TAP offices, at TAOnline.com, a website that has resources for transitioning military (**www.taonline.com/TapOffice**).

Seamless Transition Liaisons for the Severely Wounded

The VA has a long history of special efforts to bring information on benefits and services to active duty military personnel. In this case, they have worked

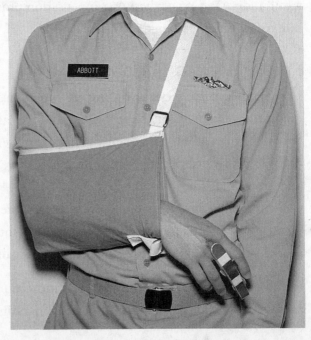

to provide a "seamless transition" for those returning from service in Operations Iraqi Freedom and Enduring Freedom. Internal coordination was improved and efforts currently focus on reducing red tape and streamlining access to all VA benefits. Each VA medical facility and regional office has identified a point of contact to coordinate activities locally to help meet the needs of these returning combat service members and veterans.

In addition, VA increased the staffing of benefits counselors at key military hospitals where severely wounded service members from Iraq and Afghanistan frequently are sent. Service members' contact with VA often begins with priority scheduling for care and, for the most seriously wounded, VA counselors visiting bedsides in military wards before separation to ensure their VA disability payment coverage will be ready the moment they leave active duty. Benefit counselors help the service member obtain VA services, and social workers facilitate health care coordination and discharge planning.

Coordinators at each VA benefits regional office and VA medical center work with counselors and with military discharge staff to ensure a smooth transition to VA services at locations nearest the veteran's residence after discharge. At the VA facilities serving the veteran's hometown, the hospital is alerted when the seriously wounded service member is being discharged so that the continuity of his or her medications and therapy is ensured when he or she arrives home. *More about transitioning back to civilian life with a disability is covered in Chapter 7.*

Checklist of Items to Complete Before You Depart the Military

This can grow to be an exhaustive list, and in general, your military service transition staff will walk you through the entire process. However, here are some key items to consider:

- **Travel** — You are entitled to travel expenses from your last permanent duty station to your place of retirement or home of record. The personnel office will instruct you on your entitlements. You are not entitled to Dislocation Allowance upon discharge or retirement.

- **Household Goods (HHG) shipment** — You are entitled to a HHG shipment from your last permanent duty station to your place of retirement or home of record. The transportation staff will assist you with this. Note that currently all HHG shipments are insured automatically at full-placement value. Now, moving companies can be liable for up to $5,000 per shipment, or $4 multiplied by the net weight of the shipment in pounds, up to $50,000, whichever is greater. Weight does not become a factor until a shipment goes over the $5,000 threshold.

- **Final pay / retirement pay** — Your personnel office will have computed your final pay and/or retirement pay benefits. Keep your current direct deposit accounts open until your transition pay/retirement pay is processed. Shifting banks during retirement is often problematic when it comes to getting your pay and travel in a timely manner.

- **Health insurance** — This is covered in depth later in this book; however, you should have been counseled on your entitlements.

- **Complete medical physical** — You *must* have a physical before discharge or retirement. This is your last chance to document any ailments, injuries, chronic pain, problems, or illnesses before you depart active duty. It is highly recommended that you document everything while on active duty, as it is much more difficult to connect service-related injuries/disabilities after you depart the military without any significant documentation on your active duty health record. Make sure you get a complete copy of your health record before you depart.

- **Dental care** — This is an area that leaves quite a bit to be desired. Even the retiree dental plan (discussed later) is not great. Typically, you are eligible for one dental exam and treatment in a VA dental facility. To obtain this, you must apply within 90 days of your discharge date, and the actual treatment must be completed within 180 days from your discharge date.

- **Terminal leave and administrative absence** — Retirement is the only time officers can sell leave; however, all service members may take terminal leave (at command discretion) when departing the military. You also are authorized (with command approval) up to 21 days of administrative absence in connection with retirement. This is subject to rules, which differ by each military service, and is designed to give you additional time to transition to civilian life. You will need to determine and calculate the benefits of selling leave versus terminal leave (or a combination of both). You also might be eligible for Retirement Processing Point (RPP), which authorizes you to depart your permanent duty station and report to the closest unit to your retirement for purposes of easing the transition to retirement. This is authorized at command discretion, and of course, there must be a unit (for your service) within a reasonable commuting distance of your desired retirement location.

- **Permissive orders** — Most services allow for up to five days of permissive orders for house or job seeking. However, this is not allowed in conjunction with administrative absence, travel, or terminal leave and is entirely at the expense of the service member.

This is a short list of some of the main issues you will need to understand before you depart the military, but there are obviously many more. All should be thoroughly presented and discussed by your transition and personnel/administration staff and understood by you.

Veterans' Preference

Many of you will be entering the civilian workforce and/or applying for government civil service positions when you finish your time in the military. It is important that you understand what your veterans' preferences are before you begin the process of job-hunting. Veterans' preference can improve your odds of competing for jobs greatly, particularly for civil service positions.

Why preference is given

Since the time of the Civil War, veterans of the Armed Forces have been given some degree of preference in appointments to federal jobs. Recognizing their sacrifice, Congress enacted laws to prevent veterans seeking federal employment from being penalized for their time in military service. Veterans' preference recognizes the economic loss suffered by citizens who have served their country in uniform, restores veterans to a favorable competitive position for government employment, and acknowledges the larger obligation owed to disabled veterans.

Veterans' preference in its present form comes from the Veterans' Preference Act of 1944. By law, veterans who are disabled or who served on active duty in the Armed Forces during certain specified periods or in military campaigns are entitled to preference over others in hiring from competitive lists of eligibles and in retention during reductions in force.

In addition to receiving preference in competitive appointments, veterans may be considered for special noncompetitive appointments for which only they are eligible.

When preference applies

Preference in hiring applies to permanent and temporary positions in the competitive and excepted services of the executive branch. Preference does not apply to positions in the Senior Executive Service or to executive branch positions for which Senate confirmation is required. The legislative and judicial branches of the federal government also are exempt from the Veterans' Preference Act unless the positions are in the competitive service (Government Printing Office, for example) or have been made subject to the act by another law.

Preference applies in hiring from civil service examinations conducted by the Office of Personnel Management (OPM) and agencies under delegated examining authority for most excepted service jobs including Veterans Recruitment Appointments (VRA) and when agencies make temporary, term, and overseas limited appointments. Veterans' preference does not apply to promotion, reassignment, change to lower grade, transfer, or reinstatement.

Veterans' preference does not require an agency to use any particular appointment process. Agencies have broad authority under law to hire from any appropriate source of eligibles including special appointing authorities. An agency may consider candidates already in the civil service from an agency-developed merit promotion list, or it may reassign a current employee, transfer an employee from another agency, or reinstate a former federal employee. In addition, agencies are required to give priority to displaced employees before using civil service examinations and similar hiring methods.

Types of preference

The National Defense Authorization Act for fiscal year 2006 clarified the scope of the term "veteran" for the purposes of determining who is entitled to veterans' preference. To receive preference, a veteran must have been discharged or released from active duty in the Armed Forces under honorable conditions (i.e., with an honorable or general discharge).

Military retirees at the rank of major, lieutenant commander, or higher are not eligible for preference in appointment unless they are disabled veterans. This does not apply to reservists who will not begin drawing military retired pay until age 60.

For nondisabled users, active duty for training by National Guard or Reserve soldiers does not qualify as "active duty" for preference. For disabled veterans, active duty includes training service in the Reserves or National Guard.

When applying for federal jobs, eligible veterans should claim preference on their application or résumé.

5-Point Preference (TP)

A veteran is eligible to receive a couple levels of preference. Five points are added to the passing examination score (or rating for a civil service position application) of a veteran who served:

- During a war
- During the period April 28, 1952, through July 1, 1955
- For more than 180 consecutive days, other than for training, any part of which occurred after January 31, 1955, and before October 15, 1976
- During the Gulf War from August 2, 1990, through January 2, 1992
- For more than 180 consecutive days, other than for training, any part of which occurred during the period beginning September 11, 2001, and ending on the date prescribed by presidential proclamation or by law as the last day of Operation Iraqi Freedom
- In a campaign or expedition for which a campaign medal has been authorized. Any Armed Forces Expeditionary medal or campaign badge, including El Salvador, Lebanon, Grenada, Panama, Southwest Asia, Somalia, and Haiti, qualifies for preference.

A campaign medal holder or Gulf War veteran who originally enlisted after September 7, 1980, (or began active duty on or after October 14, 1982, and has not previously completed 24 months of continuous active duty) must have served continuously for 24 months or the full period called or ordered to active duty.

A service member whose record appears to show service qualifying for Veterans' preference (for example, there is an indication that the person served in Bosnia in 1996), may be accorded five points tentative preference on that basis alone. However, before the person can be appointed, he or she must submit proof of entitlement to preference. That proof may be an amended DD Form 214 showing the award of the Armed Forces Expeditionary Medal (AFEM) for Bosnia in the case of service members who served there and were released before enactment of the recent Veterans' preference amendments, or it may be other official documentation showing award of the Armed Forces Expeditionary Medal. These additional five points give you significant advantage in the hiring and selection process over other non-veterans; however, it is not a guarantee of employment.

Gulf War Preference

The Defense Authorization Act of Fiscal Year 1998 (Public Law 105-85) of November 18, 1997, contains a provision (section 1102 of Title XI) which accords Veterans' preference to everyone who served on active duty during the period beginning August 2, 1990, and ending January 2, 1992, provided, of course, the veteran is otherwise eligible.

This means that anyone who served on active duty during the Gulf War, regardless of where or for how long, is entitled to preference if otherwise eligible (i.e., have been separated under honorable conditions and served continuously for a minimum of 24 months or the full period for which called or ordered to active duty). This applies not only to candidates seeking employment, but to federal employees who may be affected by reduction in force, as well.

The law specifies that only those on active duty during the period beginning August 2, 1990, and ending January 2, 1992, are eligible for preference. Applicants who served on active duty exclusively after these dates would have to be in receipt of a campaign badge or expeditionary medal.

For example, someone who enlisted in the Army and was serving on active duty when the Gulf War broke out on Aug 2, 1990, would have to complete a minimum of 24 months service to be eligible for preference. On the other hand, a reservist who was called to active duty for a month and spent all his time at the Pentagon before being released also would be eligible.

10-Point Compensable Disability Preference (CP)

Ten points are added to the passing examination score or rating of a veteran who:

- Served at any time and who has a compensable service-connected disability rating of at least 10 percent but less than 30 percent. *Refer back to Chapter 1 for information on the disability ratings.*

- Served at any time and who has a compensable service-connected disability rating of 30 percent or more

- Served at any time and has a present service-connected disability or is receiving compensation, disability retirement benefits, or pension from the military or the Department of Veterans Affairs but does not qualify as a CP or CPS or a veteran who received a Purple Heart

Applicants claiming 10-point preference must complete Standard Form (SF) 15 (**www.opm.gov/forms/pdf_fill/sf15.pdf**) and submit the requested documentation.

10-Point Derived Preference (XP)

Ten points are added to the passing examination score or rating of spouses, widows, widowers, or mothers of veterans as described below. This type of preference usually is referred to as "derived preference" because it is based on service of a veteran who is not able to use the preference.

A mother and a spouse (including widow or widower) may be entitled to preference based on the same veteran's service if they both meet the requirements. However, neither may receive preference if the veteran is living and is qualified for federal employment.

Spouse

Ten points are added to the passing examination score or rating of the spouse of a disabled veteran who is disqualified for a federal position along the general lines of his or her usual occupation because of a service-connected disability. Such a disqualification may be presumed when the veteran is unemployed and:

- Is rated by appropriate military or Department of Veterans Affairs authorities to be 100 percent disabled and/or unemployable

- Has retired, been separated, or resigned from a civil service position on the basis of a disability that is service-connected in origin

- Has attempted to obtain a civil service position or other position along the lines of his or her usual occupation and has failed to qualify because of a service-connected disability

Preference may be allowed in other circumstances, but anything less than the above warrants a more careful analysis.

NOTE: Veterans' preference for spouses is different than the preference the Department of Defense is required by law to extend to spouses of active duty members in filling its civilian positions. For more information on that program, contact the Department of Defense.

Widow / Widower

Ten points are added to the passing examination score or rating of the widow or widower of a veteran who was not divorced from the veteran or has not remarried. If he or she did remarry, the remarriage had to have been annulled. The veteran either:

- Served during a war or during the period April 28, 1952, through July 1, 1955, or in a campaign or expedition for which a campaign medal has been authorized

- Died while on active duty that included service described immediately above under conditions that would not have been the basis for other than an honorable or general discharge

Mother of a veteran

Ten points are added to the passing examination score or rating of the mother of a veteran who died under honorable conditions while on active duty during a war or during the period April 28, 1952, through July 1, 1955, or in a campaign or expedition for which a campaign medal has been authorized. This also applies to the mother of a living disabled veteran if the veteran was separated with an honorable or general discharge from active duty, including training service in the Reserves or National Guard, performed at any time and is permanently and totally disabled from a service-connected injury or illness. The mother:

- Is or was married to the father of the veteran
- Lives with her permanently disabled husband (either the veteran's father or her husband through remarriage)

- Is widowed, divorced, or separated from the veteran's father and has not remarried
- Remarried but is widowed, divorced, or legally separated from her husband when she claims preference

Note: The widow or mother of a deceased disabled veteran who served after 1955, but did not serve in a war, campaign, or expedition, would not be entitled to preference.

The "rule of three" and veteran passovers

Selection must be made from the highest three eligibles on the certificate who are available for the job — the "rule of three." However, an agency may not pass over a preference eligible to select a lower ranking nonpreference eligible or nonpreference eligible with the same or lower score.

Example: If the top person on a certificate is a 10-point disabled veteran (CP or CPS) and the second and third persons are 5-point preference eligibles, the appointing authority may choose any of the three.

If the top person on a certificate is a 10-point disabled veteran (CP or CPS), the second person is not a preference eligible, and the third person is a 5-point preference eligible, the appointing authority may choose either of the preference eligibles. The appointing authority may not pass over the 10-point disabled veteran to select the nonpreference eligible unless an objection has been sustained.

Chapter 3

Military Retirement

ne of the biggest incentives to join the military is its robust retirement benefit package. You are eligible for retirement after just 20 years of service, which means an individual who signs up at 18 can retire at age 38. There are several retirement plans, determined by the date you entered active duty service. *More information on medical retirement and medical discharges will be covered at the end of this chapter.* With the state of our economy, there is much talk about reducing military retirement benefits, delaying retirement benefit payments until a certain age, and even eliminating many retirement benefits. With any luck, our government officials will continue to honor the commitment given to each of us when we joined the military despite discussions about changing the military retirement system.

How you request your retirement is based on service specific policy, but typically, retirement requests may be submitted anytime a member is retirement eligible — usually no more than one year in advance, nor less than six months in advance of the requested retirement date. Once approved by your service, you are issued retirement "orders" that contain the accounting information, retirement date, and specific instructions to prepare for your retirement. Here is a list of some of the items you will have to consider and complete:

- **Counseling** — Before your retirement, it is important that you participate in briefings, counseling sessions, and administrative guidance and, of course, attend a Transition Assistance Program (TAP). *Refer back to Chapter 2 for information about TAP.* The decisions you make at the time of retirement directly affect your entitlements, benefits, and the amount of your pay and survivor benefits. You will find some decisions, once made, are impossible to change, so give careful thought and consideration to this, and take the time to discuss your options with family.

- **Documentation** — Your documents form the basis for the establishment of your retired account and are to be completed as part of your preretirement preparation. This is, of course, service specific, and your branch of service may have unique different forms and/or procedures.

- **Allotment Authorization** — You can start, stop, or change current allotments by requesting action by the office that takes care of your active duty pay account. Ensure your allotment total will not exceed your retirement pay. All necessary adjustment to your allotments should be made at least 30 days before retirement.

- **Payment Method/Schedule** — Your net retired/retainer pay should be sent to your financial institution by direct deposit unless you live in a foreign country in which direct deposit is not available. Your retired pay will be deposited to your account on the first business day of the month following the end of the month. Direct deposit enables your payment to be deposited directly to the bank, saving and loan association, or credit union of your choice.

How Retirement Pay is Calculated

Navy and Marine Corps members are considered a retired member for classification purposes if you are an enlisted member with more than 30 years of service or are a warrant or commissioned officer. Enlisted Navy and Marine Corps members with less than 30 years of service are transferred to the Fleet Reserve/Fleet Marine Corps Reserve, and their pay is referred to as "retainer pay." Air Force, Army, and Coast Guard members with more than 20 years service all are classified as retired. When a Navy or Marine Corps member completes 30 years, including time on the retired rolls in receipt of retainer pay, the Fleet Reserve status is changed to retired status. Retired pay amounts are determined by multiplying your service factor (normally referred to as your multiplier) by your active duty base pay at the time of retirement Base Pay at Time of Retirement). By law, the gross retired pay must be rounded down to a whole dollar amount.

(1) Service Factor (Multiple)

If you are a retiree with 30 or more years of service, your multiple is 75 percent. If you are a retiree/Fleet Reservist with less than 30 years, this factor is determined by taking 2 ½ percent times your years of service. Years of service include credit for each full month of service as $1/12$th of a year. Years of service for officers includes all active service, periods of inactive reserve service before June 1, 1958, ROTC active duty time before October 13, 1964, constructive service credit for Medical and Dental Corps, and drills performed while in the inactive reserve after May 31, 1958. Years of service for Fleet Reservists and all other enlisted retirements include all active service, active duty for training performed after August 9, 1956, any constructive service earned for a minority, or short-term enlistment completed before December 31, 1977, and includes drills performed while in the Active Reserves.

(2) Base Pay at Time of Retirement

If you entered the service before September 8, 1980, your base pay for retirement is the same as your last active duty pay. (Remember, your allowances are not considered). An example of this type of retired pay calculations is as follows:

- A Navy or Marine E-8 is transferring to Fleet Reserve on July 31, 2000, with 22 years, eight months service.
- 2.5 percent x 22.67 years = 56.68 percent.
- 56.68 percent x $3161.10 (July 1, 2000, active duty rate for an E-8 over 22 years) = $1791.71 or $1,791.00 per month.

For those who entered the Armed Forces on or after September 8, 1980, the base pay is the average of the highest 36 months of active duty base pay received. The base pay for members having less than three years service is the average monthly active duty basic pay during their period of service. For certain retirees who entered the Armed Forces on or after September 8, 1980, the initial cost-of-living increase is reduced.

- For those who entered the Armed Forces on or after August 1, 1986, the base pay is computed the same way as it is computed for retirees identified in section (2) above. However, there may be differences in how cost-of-living increases are computed between the services. Check with your branch of the military for specifics.

Tower Amendment

In addition to the computation explained previously, your pay will be computed according to provisions of the Tower Amendment if it applies to your situation. The Tower Amendment was enacted to ensure you would not receive a lesser amount of retired pay than you would have received if you had retired on a prior date. The Tower eligibility date is usually the day before the effective date of an active duty pay increase. Tower pay is computed by using the active duty pay rates in effect on that date, your rank/rate on that date, total service accumulated on that date, and all applicable cost-of-living increases.

(1) Using the previous example, the member had a rank of E-8 and had 22 years and one month of service on December 31, 1999. The member's pay would be computed as follows:

- 2.5 percent x 22.08 years = 55.20 percent.
- 55.20 percent x $3,119.40 (January 1, 1998, active duty rate for an E-8 over 22 years) = $1,721.90 + 2.8 percent (COLA Increase) = $1,769.00

(2) Because the E-8 was eligible to transfer to the Fleet Reserve on December 31, 1998, they also would compute the entitlement as of that date. The E-8 has 21 years, 1 month service. The pay would be computed as follows:

- 2.5 percent x 21.08 = 52.70 percent
- 52.70 percent x $2,976.60 (1/1/99 active duty rate for an E-8 over 21 years) = $1,568.00 + 1.3 percent (COLA Increase) = $1,588.00 + 2.8 percent (COLA Increase) = $1,632.00

(3) In this situation therefore, this Fleet Reservist would receive monthly retainer pay of $1,796.00 because the Tower Amendment computations are not more beneficial than the current pay computation.

You can estimate your monthly retirement pay at **www.defenselink.mil/militarypay/retirement/calc/index.html**.

Military Stop-Loss

Presidential authority may suspend any provision of law pertaining to separation and retirement from the military. In other words, the military legally may keep you in uniform past your planned separation or retirement dates in times of national emergency. Stop-loss implementation authority was delegated to the secretary of defense by executive order on Sept. 14, 2001. It was, in turn, delegated to the secretaries of the services.

A stop-loss order can affect an entire branch of service or specific military operations. At one time or another in the past few years, members of all services have had their terms of service extended to meet operational requirements.

Retirement System Choices

To decide which system applies to you, you must determine the date that you first entered the military. This date is called the DIEMS (Date of Initial Entry to Military Service) or DIEUS (Date of Initial Entry to Uniformed Services). The date you first entered the military is the first time you enlisted or joined the active or Reserves. This date is fixed — it does not change. Departing the military and rejoining does not affect your DIEMS.

Some individuals have unique circumstances that complicate determining their DIEMS. Here are a few examples:

- The DIEMS for academy graduates who entered the academy with no prior service is the date they reported to the academy, not the date they graduated.

- Beginning an ROTC scholarship program or enlisting as a reserve in the Senior ROTC program sets the DIEMS, not the graduation or commissioning date.

- Members who entered the military, separated, and then rejoined the military have a DIEMS based on entering the first period of military service.

- The DIEMS for members who enlisted under the delayed entry program is the date they entered the delayed entry program, not when they initially reported for duty.

- For those who joined the Reserves and later joined the active component, their DIEMS is the date they joined the Reserves.

Be aware that your pay date may be different than your DIEMS. Also, your DIEMS does not determine when you have enough time in the service to retire. It only determines which retirement system applies to you.

Not all services have their DIEMS dates properly defined in their personnel records. If you have unusual circumstances and are unsure of when your DIEMS date is or believe your records show an incorrect DIEMS date, contact your personnel office to discuss your particular situation.

Based upon the date you initially entered the military, you can determine which retirement system applies to you. For the Final Pay and High-3 systems, each year of service is worth 2.5 percent toward the retirement multiplier. Hence, 2.5 percent x 20 years = 50 percent and 2.5 percent x 30 years = 75 percent. The longer an individual stays on active duty, the higher the multiplier and the higher the retirement pay, up to the maximum of 100 percent of basic pay for 40 years of service.

Remember that only basic pay is used in retirement calculations. Allowances and special pays do not affect retired pay.

Cost of Living Adjustments (COLAs) are given annually based on the increase in the Consumer Price Index (CPI), a measure of inflation. Under the Final Pay and High-3 systems, the annual COLA is equal to CPI. This is a different index than the one used for active duty annual pay raises. The index used for active duty pay raises are based upon average civilian wage increases. Thus, retirement pay COLAs and annual active duty pay raises will differ.

Retirement System	Criteria to Receive
Final Pay	Entry before September 8, 1980
High-3	Entry on or after September 8, 1980, but before August 1, 1986, or entered on or after August 1, 1986, and did not choose the Career Status Bonus and REDUX retirement system

Retirement System	Criteria to Receive
CSB/REDUX	Entered on or after August 1, 1986, *and* elected to receive the Career Status Bonus (if you do not elect to receive the Career Status Bonus, you will be under the High-3 retirement system)

Retirement System	Basis	Multiplier	COLA	Bonus
Final Pay	Last Month's Basic Pay	2.5% for each Year of Service	CPI	No
High 36	Average of the Highest 36 Months Basic Pay	2.5% for each Year of Service	CPI	No
CSB REDUX	Average of the Highest 36 Months Basic Pay	3.5% for each Year over 20	CPI - 1%	Yes

Final Pay retirement system

Final Pay applies to those who entered the service before September 8, 1980.

Years of service	20	21	22	23	24	25	26	27	28	29	30
Final Pay	50%	52.5%	55%	57.5%	60%	62.5%	65%	67.5%	70%	72.5%	75%

This multiplier is applied against the final basic pay of the individual's career.

High-3 Year Average retirement system

This system applies to members who first entered the service after September 8, 1980, but before August 1, 1986. It also applies to individuals who entered on or after August 1, 1986, who do not elect the REDUX retirement system with the Career Status Bonus at their 15th year of service.

Years of service	20	21	22	23	24	25	26	27	28	29	30
High-3	50%	52.5%	55%	57.5%	60%	62.5%	65%	67.5%	70%	72.5%	75%

This multiplier is applied against the average basic pay for the highest 36 months of the individual's career. This typically, though not always, equals the average basic pay for the final three years of service.

CSB/REDUX retirement system

The Military Reform Act of 1986 created the REDUX retirement system. It applies to all members who joined on or after August 1, 1986. The National Defense Authorization Act (NDAA) in 2000 amended this system. The NDAA made two major changes: 1) It allowed those in this group to choose between the High-3 retirement system and the REDUX retirement system, and 2) it added a $30,000 Career Status Bonus as part of the REDUX retirement system.

The CSB/REDUX retirement system applies to those who entered the service on or after August 1, 1986, *and* who elected to receive the $30,000 Career Status Bonus at their 15th year of service.

The REDUX retirement system and Career Status Bonus is a package deal. The combination of these two items can be advantageous to many individuals. The REDUX portion determines retirement income (the longer one's career, the higher that income) and the $30,000 Career Status Bonus provides current cash, available for investing, major purchases, or setting up a business after retirement.

The REDUX multiplier calculation and annual cost of living adjustments differ from the other systems. Also, REDUX has a catch-up increase at age 62 that brings the REDUX retired pay back to the same amount paid under the High-3 System. REDUX is the only military retirement system with a readjustment feature.

Each of the first 20 years of service is worth 2.0 percent toward the retirement multiplier. But each year after the 20th is worth 3.5 percent. Hence, 2.0 percent x 20 years = 40 percent. But a 30-year career is computed by 2.0 percent times the first 20 years plus 3.5 percent for the ten years beyond 20, resulting in the maximum of 100 percent of basic pay for 40 years of service. The table below summarizes the initial multiplier at various years of service under REDUX.

Years of service	20	21	22	23	24	25	26	27	28	29	30
High-3	40%	43.5%	47%	50.5%	54%	57.5%	61%	64.5%	68%	71.5%	75%

Under REDUX, the longer an individual stays on active duty, the closer the multiplier is to what it would have been under High-3 up to the 30-year point where the multipliers are equal. In precisely the same way as High-3, this multiplier is applied against the average basic pay for the highest 36 months of the individual's basic pay. This typically, though not always, equals the average basic pay for the final three years of service. Under REDUX, the COLA is equal to CPI minus 1 percent.

A feature unique to REDUX is a recomputation of retirement pay at age 62. Two adjustments are made. The first adjusts the multiplier to what it would have been under High-3. For example, a 20-year retiree's new multiplier would become 50 percent, a 24-year retiree's multiplier would become 60 percent, but a 30-year retiree's would remain 75 percent. This new multiplier is applied against the individual's original average basic pay for his or her highest 36 months. Then the second adjustment is done. Full CPI for every retirement year is applied to this amount to compute a new base retirement salary. At age 62, the REDUX and High-3 retirement salaries are equal. But, REDUX COLAs for later years will again be set at CPI minus 1 percent.

Those members who elected to follow the CSB/REDUX retirement system receive a $30,000 Career Status Bonus at their 15th year of service. To receive this bonus, the member must agree to complete a 20-year active duty career with length-of-service retired pay under the 1986 Military Retirement Reform Act — 1986 MRRA or REDUX. Continuation beyond 20 years is possible, subject to service personnel management actions. However, the member's commitment to the CSB is only to the 20-year point. The entire $30,000 bonus, or first installment payment for those electing a multi-year payment option, is paid shortly after the member makes the CSB/REDUX election and commits to the 20-years-of-service obligation.

(Exact mechanics should be provided by your service when you have about 14.5 years of service.)

This $30,000 is taxable unless placed into the Thrift Savings Plan (TSP) or other qualified investment. Under current rules, you may place a maximum of $10,500 in a TSP account. Taxes would not be paid on this $10,500 or its earnings until withdrawal.

If the member does not complete the obligation of the 20-year career, the member must repay a prorated share of the bonus.

Making the choice

If you are a service member who entered the service after July 31, 1986, you can choose between the High-3 and REDUX options. Both have their own merits. Neither is universally better than the other. Only you can choose which option will be more advantageous to your situation.

The following fictitious story from the U.S. Department of Defense website at **www.defense.gov** about twin brothers Harry and Richard shows the differences between the High-3 and CSB/REDUX retirement systems, the potential worth of the Career Status Bonus, and insight of the lifetime value of the two retirement options.

In August 1986, Harry and Richard, 20-year-old twins, enlisted in the military. As Harry and Richard had always done everything together, they continued to do so by being promoted with identical dates for their entire career. But, one event is about to make their careers and futures different.

In 2001, Harry and Richard face a choice. They are nearing their 15th year of service and may retain the High-3 retirement plan or they may take a $30,000 Career Status Bonus and the REDUX retirement system. Harry chose High-3 and Richard chose the single lump sum CSB/REDUX option. Immediately, their finances changed. Richard now had $30,000 more in cash. This money was his to spend as he wished — a down payment on a house, college tuition for the kids, a new car, or invest for use later.

Richard decided not to invest in the TSP but instead to pay tax on the entire amount now and invest the entire after-tax balance in a mutual fund earning 8 percent annually. As the $30,000 is taxable income and Richard is in the 28-percent tax bracket, he will pay $8,400 in taxes on this bonus, leaving $21,600 to invest.

In 2006, Harry and Richard retire with 20 years of service. Because they both had an average (highest three years) base pay of $3,000 per month, Harry, under High-3, gets 50 percent or $1,500 per month, and Richard, under REDUX, gets 40 percent or $1,200. Although Harry has a larger retirement check than Richard, Richard has been building up the savings on his $21,600 of Career Status Bonus for the past five years, and it is now worth $28,600 (after paying taxes on its earnings).

Each year during their retirement, Harry and Richard will receive cost-of-living adjustments (COLAs) based upon the consumer price index (CPI), which measures inflation. Harry's High-3 COLA is the full CPI (3.5 percent each year in our story), so Harry gets a 3.5 percent raise. Richard, however, gets a 2.5 percent raise because COLAs under the REDUX system are equal to CPI minus 1 percent. But, Richard's Career Status Bonus is still growing in his mutual fund.

This story continues the same way until 2028 as they near their 62nd birthday. Up to this point, Harry has received nearly $582,000 in retirement income, and his current monthly amount is now about $3,100. Richard has collected $415,000 total and now gets a bit more than $2,000 each month. But, Richard is still saving that Career Status Bonus. It is now worth $98,000. Counting both the mutual fund value and what he's collected in retirement, selecting the CSB/REDUX plan netted him $513,600 — close, but $68,300 less than Harry has received.

Their 62nd birthday also brings retirement adjustment for Richard. Richard's retirement pay is recomputed as if he had been under High-3 all these years. This means that he will now get 50 percent of his original base pay plus full 3.5 percent COLAs added to it for his past retirement years. So, for one year, Harry and Richard receive the exact same retirement pay —

about $3,200 per month. This is for only one year because the following year, Harry gets his 3.5 percent COLA and Richard gets his 2.5 percent COLA, but it is added to his newly adjusted retirement salary of $3,200. This "catch-up" adjustment impacts Richard's total accumulation, and by the end of the year, his total is within $63,000 of Harry's total accumulation. The following year Richard's total retirement accumulation and the balance of his mutual fund begin to surpass Harry's total accumulation.

By now, some people would have spent some or all of the money Richard put in the mutual fund on vacations, cars, or to augment their retirement income, but Richard wants to pass the money to his heirs and keeps saving. When they are 75, Harry has received more than $1,260,000 in retirement income; his current monthly amount is $5,000. Richard has collected more than $1,049,000 in retirement income and now earns $4,400 each month. But, Richard is still saving that Career Status Bonus — it is worth more than $214,600. Counting both the mutual fund value and what he has collected in retirement, selecting the CSB/REDUX retirement option is worth $1,264,000, surpassing Harry's total amount by $4,000. From this point forward, Richard will continue to outpace Harry's total accumulation.

The following chart summarizes Harry and Richard's story. Remember that this is an example that shows the differences between the CSB/REDUX and High-3 options. These results are dependent upon the assumptions built into the story and the choices that Richard made.

Point of Comparison	Harry (High-3)	Richard (CSB/REDUX)
15th Year of Service		
Bonus	$0	$30,000
Taxes	$0	-$8,400
Total	$0	$21,600
Time of Retirement		
Savings	$0	$28,600
Cumulative retired pay	$0	$0

Point of Comparison	Harry (High-3)	Richard (CSB/REDUX)
Total	$0	$28,600
End of First Retirement Year		
Savings Cumulative retired pay	$0 $18,000	$30,200 $14,400
Total	$18,000	$44,600
Retirement pay for the year	$18,800	$14,400
Age 61		
Savings Cumulative retired pay	$0 $581,000	$98,000 $415,600
Total	$581,000	$513,600
Retirement pay for the year	$37,100	$24,200
Age 62 — REDUX Readjustment		
Savings Cumulative retired pay	$0 $620,300	$103,600 $454,000
Total	$620,300	$557,600
Retirement pay for the year	$38,400	$38,400
Age 75		
Savings Cumulative retired pay	$0 $1,260,000	$214,600 $1,049,000
Total	$1,260,000	$1,264,000
Retirement pay for the year	$60,000	$52,900

Many individual differences — age, salary, years of service at retirement, spending and saving habits — will and should influence your decision and will make your story with a fictitious twin different than Harry and Richard's. A calculator that allows you to enter your personal situation is available at **www.defenselink.mil/militarypay/retirement/calc/04_ compare.html**.

Temporary Early Retirement Authorization (TERA)

A law has been passed that grants all branches of service temporary authority to approve retirements for members with more than 15 but less than 20 years of service. This is also known as the Voluntary Separation Incentive Program and has not been authorized by law since 2001. In order to compute retired pay under this provision of law, a retiree is assessed a reduction factor. The reduction factor is computed as 1 minus one twelve hundredth of the difference between 240 (the number of months for a standard 20 year retirement) and the number of months of creditable service for retired pay. The reduction factor is assessed upon the standard retired pay computation, which provides for 2.5 percent for each year of service, multiplied by the final base pay on active duty or the average of the highest 36 months of base pay.

Changes to Your Pay and Retirement Benefits

Just as civilians are subject to changes in their retirement benefits in the form of taxes, Social Security, and other deductions and compensations, retired military also must be prepared to have their retirement pay adjusted, whether for good or bad, for inflation, higher taxes, and other changes. This section will detail many of these deductions and increases and will help you better prepare your financial future after your military career has finished.

Deductions to retired pay

Military retirement pay is not exempt from taxes and other withholdings. You will see the following deductions to your pay:

(1) Federal withholding tax — In most cases, retired pay is fully taxable. Survivor benefit plan (SBP) costs and any waiver for VA compensation reduce the amount of taxable income. The amount deducted from your pay for federal withholding tax is based on the number of exemptions you indicate on either your pay data form or your W-4 after retirement. To change your withholding tax status or to request an additional withholding amount after retirement, forward an IRS Form W-4 to DFAS or the Coast Guard Personnel Service Center, as appropriate.

Disability retirement payments are taxable for those members with either total military service after September 24, 1975, or who were in the service before this date but were not on active military service or under binding written commitment to become a member of the armed services on September 24, 1975. Disability retirement payments are nontaxable for those members with total military service before September 24, 1975; these members were on active military duty or under binding written commitment to a member of the armed services on September 24, 1975. Or, their disability retirement has been deemed combat related, regardless of their active military service.

The amount of taxable income may be reduced further by any SBP cost. If, after retirement, you waive a portion of your pay in favor of VA compensation, your taxable income will be reduced by the amount of VA compensation or the amount of percentage of disability calculation, whichever is greater. *VA compensation will be covered in Chapter 7.*

(2) State withholding tax — State tax withholding is on a voluntary basis and must be in whole dollar amounts. The minimum monthly amount is $10. Before making your request in writing, you must contact the taxing authority in the state in which you have established residence to determine if you are required to pay state income tax.

(3) Federal Insurance Contribution Act (Social Security) — Retired/ retainer pay is not subject to FICA deductions, nor is your retired pay reduced when you become entitled to Social Security payments.

Changes in benefits and entitlements

Even though your retirement benefits should be consistent based on the systems explained in the last section, several categories of changes might affect how much you receive or what your other benefits provide for you. Remember that some of these changes might entitle you to more money, not less. Here are some things to pay attention to:

Tax levies — If you owe money to the Internal Revenue Service (IRS), your retirement pay may be affected. A tax levy is a legal seizure of your property or assets to satisfy a tax debt. All services, including military retirement, must honor tax levies for delinquent taxes issued by the IRS. As in the case of garnishments, the collection action is mandatory, and any rebuttal concerning the levy must be addressed to the IRS. Levies will run until the entire amount either is collected or the IRS informs your servicing pay office that it is released from collecting the levy amount.

Cost-of-living increases — Current provisions of law authorize periodic increases to retired pay. These increases were intended to reflect rises in the Consumer Price Index (CPI). The increases affect the amounts of gross monthly pay, federal withholding tax, survivor benefit plan costs, and annuities. Retired members who entered the Armed Forces on or after September 8, 1980, and who became entitled to retired pay on or after January 1, 1996, will receive an initial cost-of-living increase computed, using the quarter of the retirement date, minus 1 percent. Cost-of-living increases thereafter for members meeting the above conditions will be unreduced. Cost-of-living increases for retired members who entered the Armed Forces on or after August 1, 1986, will be reduced by 1 percent.

Annual Cost-of-Living Adjustment

A proposed cost-of-living increase is included in the president's budget proposal released early each calendar year. It is part of the spending forecast and appropriations request for the ensuing fiscal year, a starting point for legislative discussion. However, the actual percentage increase is set through a separate bill debated by Congress and usually signed into law the following fall.

Legislators are not bound by any specific annual Consumer Price Index formula, but historically, they have chosen to mirror the percentage given to Social Security recipients. The Social Security increase, in turn, is based on a Bureau of Labor Statistics calculation of the rise in the consumer price index for urban wage earners and clerical workers (CPI-W).

Cost-of-living adjustments become effective December 1 each year and are reflected in the payment received by veterans on or about the first day of the new year. Whenever a payment falls on a holiday or weekend, as is the case with the January 1 payment each year, that month's payment is issued the last prior business day.

Federal civil service retirement — If you subsequently retire from federal civilian service and wish to waive your military retired pay (to include your military service in the computation of your civil service annuity), you must contact your servicing pay office, in writing, at least 60 days before your planned civilian retirement date. It is suggested that you contact your civilian personnel office before the submission of your waiver request to ensure that you are aware of all the available options. If you elect survivor coverage from your civil service annuity, your military SBP participation will be suspended while you receive the civil service annuity. If you want to retain military SBP, you may do so, but you must then decline survivor annuity from the Office of Personnel Management. If your pay is subject to court-ordered distribution, you must authorize an allotment in an amount equal to the distribution in order to include military service in the civil service annuity computation.

Garnishment — Your retired pay is subject to garnishment for payment of child support or alimony upon the issue of a writ of garnishment by a state or federal court. Any action to rebut the writ of garnishment or to restrain its execution must be taken through the court that issued it.

Payments to a Former Spouse — Your retired pay is subject to court-ordered distribution to a spouse or former spouse when the parties were married to each other for at least ten years during which you performed at least ten years of creditable military service. The distribution can consist of a division of disposable retired pay and may include community property or payments of alimony and/or child support. The total amount payable under this provision of law cannot exceed 50 percent of the disposable retired pay. In cases in which there is both a division of pay and a garnishment, the total amount payable cannot exceed 65 percent of the disposable retired pay. You will be notified should a distribution be applied to your retired pay. Any action to rebut the court order or to restrain its execution must be taken through the court that issued it. Payment is not automatic. Former spouses must apply to your pay office to receive this benefit.

Combat-Related Special Compensation (CRSC)

If you were involved in any of the combat periods specified in Chapter 1 of this book, you might qualify for some additional funds for your sacrifice

for your country, which are designed to compensate you for the reduction of your military retired pay due to the receipt of Department of Veterans Affairs (VA) compensation (also known as the VA waivers). With CRSC, you can receive either partial or full concurrent receipt of your military retirement pay and your VA disability compensation.

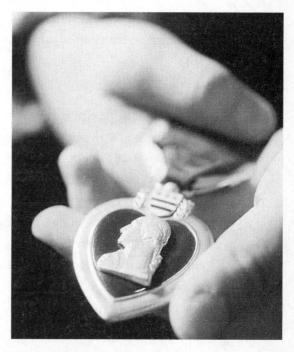

CRSC pay is based on the combined disability rating of combat-related disabilities as determined by your branch of service. *More about disability ratings and VA compensation will be discussed in Chapter 7.* Only combat-related disabilities for which you actually receive VA compensation will be considered. Use the following formula to obtain your combined VA rating of multiple combat-related disabilities:

1. Subtract each disability percent from 100 percent to obtain the remaining efficiencies.
2. Multiply the remaining efficiencies together.

3. Subtract the result from 100 percent.
4. Round to the nearest 10 percent, round up for 5 percent or above.

Example: Using three disabilities of 50 percent, 40 percent, and 30 percent:

1. [100 - 50 = 50 percent] / [100 - 40 = 60 percent] /
   [100 - 30 = 70 percent]
2. 50 percent x 60 percent x 70 percent = 21 percent
3. 100 percent - 21 percent = 79 percent
4. 79 percent rounds up to an 80 percent combined disability.

With the inception of the CRSC program on June 1, 2003, the following eligibility requirements were established:

- Retirees must apply to their respective branch of service to be approved for CRSC.
- Retirees must be in receipt of VA compensation.
- Retirees must be in receipt of military retired pay or be in a suspended pay status due to receipt of VA compensation.
- Retirees must have an approved combat-related VA disability rating of 60 percent or greater. Retirees having an approved combat-related disability associated with a Purple Heart have to have a rating of 10 percent or greater.
- Retirees must have 20 years of active service or, for reservists, 7,200 reserve points in order to be eligible.
- Retirees who have waived their retired pay in lieu of a civil service retirement are not eligible for CRSC.

Effective January 1, 2004, CRSC eligibility was extended to retirees with combat-related VA disability ratings between 10 percent and 50 percent. Additionally, reservists needed only 20 years of qualifying service (supported by documentation from the applicable branch of service such as a 20-year letter, retirement orders, or a statement of service) in order to be eligible. The other eligibility requirements remained unchanged. Note that qualified reservists will not receive CRSC until they begin to receive retired pay at age 60.

Temporary Early Retirement Authorization (TERA) retirees are not eligible to receive CRSC unless they have returned to active duty and accumulated enough service time to meet the 20-year requirement before retiring for the second time.

Veterans whose service-connected disabilities are rated at 30 percent or more are entitled to additional allowances for dependents. Depending upon the disability rating of the veteran, monthly allowances for a spouse range from $39 to $94 and for a dependent child, $26 to $88. Additional amounts are provided for each additional child, and there is a higher scale for children in school after age 18.

Social Security

While you are in military service, you pay Social Security taxes just as civilian employees do. For 2013, the maximum taxable earnings amount for Social Security is $110,100. The Social Security tax (OASDI) rate for wages paid in 2013 is 4.2 percent for employees and 6.2 percent for employers. For example, an individual with wages equal to or more than $113,700 would contribute $4,775.40 to Social Security in 2013. The employer would contribute $7,049.40. If you earn more, you continue to pay the Medicare portion of the tax (1.45 percent) on the rest of your earnings.

To qualify for benefits, you must have worked and paid Social Security taxes for a certain length of time. In 2013, workers generally receive one credit for each $1,200 of earnings. For 2012, the amount of earnings for one credit was $1,130. A worker can receive a maximum of four credits for any year. Generally, 40 credits are needed to be eligible for benefits. The amount needed to get credit for your work goes up each year. The number of credits you need to qualify for Social Security benefits depends on your age and the type of benefit for which you are eligible. No one needs more than ten years of work.

Your Social Security benefit depends on your earnings, averaged over your working lifetime. Generally, the higher your earnings, the higher your Social Security benefit. Under certain circumstances, special earnings can be credited to your military pay record for Social Security purposes. The extra earnings are for periods of active duty or active duty for training. These extra earnings may help you qualify for Social Security or increase the amount of your Social Security benefit. Social Security will add these extra earnings to your earnings record when you file for benefits.

If you served in the military from 1940 through 1956, including attendance at a service academy, you did not pay Social Security taxes. However, you will be credited with $160 a month in earnings for military service from September 16, 1940, through December 31, 1956, if:

- You were honorably discharged after 90 or more days of service, or you were released because of a disability or injury received in the line of duty.

- You are applying for survivors benefits based on a veteran's work and the veteran died while on active duty.

You cannot receive these special credits if you are receiving a federal benefit based on the same years of service unless you were on active duty after 1956. If you were on active duty after 1956, you can get the special credit for 1951 through 1956 even if you are receiving a military retirement based on service during that period.

If you served in the military from 1957 through 1977, you are credited with $300 in additional earnings for each calendar quarter in which you received active duty basic pay. If you served in the military from 1978 through 2001, you are credited with an additional $100 in earnings, up to a maximum of $1,200 a year, for every $300 in active duty basic pay. After 2001, additional earnings are no longer credited. If you began your service after September 7, 1980, and did not complete at least 24 months of active duty or your full tour, you may not be able to receive the additional earnings.

In addition to retirement benefits, Social Security pays survivors benefits to your family when you die. You also can get Social Security benefits for you and your family if you become disabled. For more information about these benefits, ask the Social Security Administration for Understanding The Benefits (Publication No. 05-10024).

When you apply for Social Security benefits, you will be asked for proof of your military service (DD Form 214) or information about your Reserve or National Guard service.

Medicare

If you have health care insurance from the Department of Veterans Affairs or under the TRICARE or CHAMPVA program, your health benefits may change or end when you become eligible for Medicare. *See chapters 5 and 6 for more information.*

You can retire as early as age 62. But, if you do, your Social Security benefits will be reduced permanently. If you decide to apply for benefits before your full retirement age, you can work and still get some Social Security benefits. There are limits on how much you can earn without losing some or all of your retirement benefits. These limits change each year. When you apply for benefits, you will receive information about what the limits are at that time and whether work will affect your monthly benefits.

When you reach your full retirement age, you can earn as much as you are able and still get all of your Social Security benefits. Workers born before January 2, 1938, can collect full benefits at age 65. For those born after that date, the age to collect full benefits is gradually being raised to age 67. To help you decide the best time to retire, contact the Social Security Administration for a copy of Retirement Benefits (Publication No. 05-10035). Generally, there is no offset for receiving both military retirement pay and your full Social Security benefit.

Medical Retirement and Discharge

Medical retirement is significantly different than a medical discharge. In short, if you are retirement eligible but have a medical condition that prohibits you from performing your military service, you will go through a "medical board" and be medically retired, typically with a retirement and some veterans' benefits in the form of disability or other entitlements. Medical discharge is for those who are not eligible for retirement but have a medical condition that prohibits them from service on active duty. Depending on the condition and whether it is service-connected or combat-related, there may be benefits through the Department of Veterans Affairs (VA).

The process to determine medical fitness for continued duty involves two boards. One is called the Medical Evaluation Board (MEB), and the other is called the Physical Evaluation Board (PEB). Most boards are a result of a military member reporting a condition to a military hospital or military treatment facility (MTF). Under these circumstances, medical officers may require a complete physical examination of the service member to determine fitness and ultimately refer him or her to a Medical Evaluation Board when the member's medical condition or ailment renders him or her unfit for duty or incapable of performing his or her duties.

Physical or mental health issues that interrupt the performance of military duties or cause a disqualification from worldwide deployment for a period of more than 12 months will initiate a medical board. This process is the same regardless of retirement eligibility. A medical board consists of active duty (USPHS) physicians who review the clinical case file and decide whether the individual should be returned to duty or should be separated or retired from the service.

If the MEB makes the determination that a service member has a medical condition or ailment that is not compatible with continued military service, they refer the case to a Physical Evaluation Board. The PEB determines fitness and/or disability and may recommend one of the following:

- Return the member to duty (with or without assignment limitations)
- Place the member on the temporary disabled/retired list (TDRL)
- Separate the member from active duty
- Medically retire the member

The standard used by the PEB for determining fitness is whether the medical condition precludes the member from reasonably performing the duties of his or her office, grade, rank, or rating. DOD and Coast Guard have published standards for deployability and readiness, which the PEB evaluation is based upon. In all cases of a recommendation for discharge, the service member is given an appeal process with assigned legal counsel.

Determining eligibility

Four factors determine whether a service member is fit for duty, separation, permanent retirement, or temporary retirement. These are:

- Ability to perform job/rating/MOS
- Rating percentage
- Stability of the disabling condition
- Years of active service (for pre-existing conditions)

Fit for duty

The member is judged fit for duty, or able to perform his job, rating, or MOS, when he or she can reasonably perform the duties of his or her grade and military job. If the member is medically unfit to perform the duties of his or her current job, the PEB can recommend medical retraining into a job he or she will be medically qualified to perform, such as administrative type duties, although this is not common.

Once a determination of physical unfitness is made, the PEB is required by law to rate the disability using the VA Schedule for Rating Disabilities. Ratings can range from 0 to 100 percent rising in increments of 10. *This was touched on in Chapter 1 and will be covered in more detail in Chapter 7.*

Separation

If a member is judged to be unfit for duty, the PEB might rule that he or she separate from the military. This separation can take two forms: without benefits and with severance pay.

Without benefits — Separation without benefits occurs if the disability is determined to be pre-existing or not service connected, and it was not caused by or aggravated by military service. The member has less than eight years of active service. Additionally, the disability was incurred while the member was absent without leave (AWOL) or while engaged in misconduct or willful negligence. If the member has more than eight years of active service, he or she may be medically retired (if eligible) or medically separated with severance pay, even if the condition was pre-existing or hereditary. This is a key fact: After eight years of service, even if the disability is not service connected, the member may be entitled to severance pay, which will be explained by your servicing personnel office at the time of discharge.

With severance pay. Separation with disability severance pay occurs if the member is found not fit for continued military service, has less than 20 years of service (i.e. not retirement eligible), and has a disability rating of less than 30 percent. Disability severance pay equals two months basic pay for each year of service not to exceed 12 years (a maximum of 24 months basic pay). The member also may be eligible to apply for monthly disability compensation from the VA if they determine the disability is "service-connected."

Retirement

If you have been found to be physically unfit for further military service and meet certain standards specified by law, you will be granted a disability retirement. Your disability retirement may be temporary or permanent. If temporary, your status should be resolved within a five-year period.

Permanent disability retirement occurs if the member is found not fit for continued military service, the disability is determined to be permanent and stable and rated at a minimum of 30 percent, or the member has 20 years of military service.

Temporary disability retirement occurs if the member is found not fit for continued military service and is entitled to permanent disability retirement except that the disability is not stable for rating purposes (for the VA disability percentage). "Stable for rating purposes" is when the condition will likely change, degrade, or improve within the next five years — which would result in a different disability rating. When a service member is placed on the Temporary Disability Retirement List (TDRL), they must undergo a medical examination within 18 months (minimum) followed by another PEB evaluation. At that time, they may be retained on the TDRL or a final disability determination will be made.

Compensation is based on the higher of two computations: Disability rating times retired pay base, or 2.5 times years of service times retired pay base. Service members on the TDRL receive no less than 50 percent of their retired pay base. The amount of your disability-retired pay is determined by one of two methods:

- The first method is to multiply your base pay or average of highest 36 months of active duty pay at the time of retirement by the percentage of disability, which has been assigned. Members who entered the service September 8, 1980, or later must use the highest average formula. The minimum percentage for temporary disability retirees will equal 50 percent. The maximum percentage for any type of retirement is 75 percent. This computation is sometimes referred to as "Method A."

- The second method is to multiply only your years of active service at the time of your retirement by 2.5 percent by your base pay or average of highest 36 months of active duty pay at the time of retirement. This computation is sometimes referred to "Method B."

In all cases, your best source of guidance and information is through your military service. Your military treatment facility, health benefits advisers, servicing personnel and pay office, family support center, and career advisors will assist you as you navigate the Medical and Physical Evaluation Board processes and disability compensation determinations. This is a critical time for you to fight for your rights; document everything and push for your maximum benefit determination.

It is important to understand both the process of a military disability retirement or discharge and the entitlements. The actual entitlements are based on a combination of factors and are based on the policies in place at the VA for computing disability entitlements. *Chapter 7 will cover your disability benefits in detail.*

Chapter 4

Veterans Health Care and VA Hospitals

One of the main benefits veterans enjoy is access to quality health care at little or no cost through the VA network of hospitals and Medical Treatment Facilities. Since the War on Terrorism began, Military Treatment Facilities, such as the recently closed Walter Reed Army Medical Center, have enjoyed less than stellar press for the treatment of our wounded veterans. This is a travesty, which luckily was recognized and has been remedied. The next three chapters will cover, in detail, the numerous health care options available to you, your spouse, and your dependents.

The string of VA hospitals across the United States is a welcome sanctuary to our veterans who enjoy great medical care, for little or no cost. The benefit of free or low-cost access to health care for veterans is one of your biggest benefits. Understand that VA health care is not just for retirement military members. Under many other circumstances, you are entitled to VA health care, if eligible, from two years to lifetime benefits depending on how long you served, disability status, combat-related duties, and several other factors. You will be surprised at just how readily available VA facilities and VA hospitals may be.

The VA operates the nation's largest integrated health care system with more than 1,400 sites of care, including hospitals, community clinics, nursing homes, domiciliaries, readjustment counseling centers, and various other facilities. For additional information, visit the VA Web page at **www.va.gov** or **www.va.gov/health/default.asp**.

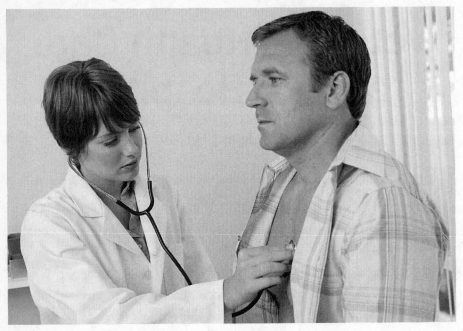

Some services provided by the VA include:

- Hospital, outpatient medical, dental, pharmacy, and prosthetic services
- Domiciliary, nursing home, and community-based residential care
- Sexual trauma counseling
- Specialized health care for women veterans
- Health and rehabilitation programs for homeless veterans
- Readjustment counseling
- Alcohol and drug dependency treatment

- Medical evaluation for disorders associated with military service in the Gulf War, or exposure to Agent Orange, radiation, and other environmental hazards

The VA will provide combat veterans free medical care for any illness possibly associated with service during a period of hostility for two years from the veteran's release from active duty.

VA Health Care Eligibility

Eligibility for most VA benefits is based upon discharge from active military service under other than dishonorable conditions. Active service means full-time service, other than active duty for training, as a member of the Army, Navy, Air Force, Marine Corps, Coast Guard, or as a commissioned officer of the Public Health Service, Environmental Science Services Administration or National Oceanic and Atmospheric Administration, or its predecessor, the Coast and Geodetic Survey. Men and women veterans with similar service may be entitled to the same VA benefits.

Current and former members of the Reserves or National Guard who were called to active duty by a federal order and completed the full period for which they were called or ordered to active duty may be eligible for VA health benefits as well. Reserves or National Guard members with active duty for training purposes only do not meet the basic eligibility requirement.

Most veterans who enlisted after September 7, 1980, or entered active duty after October 16, 1981, must have served 24 continuous months or the full period for which they were called to active duty in order to be eligible. This minimum duty requirement may not apply to veterans who were discharged for a disability incurred or aggravated in the line of duty, for a hardship or "early out," or those who served before September 7, 1980. Because there are a number of other exceptions to the minimum duty requirements, VA encourages all veterans to apply to determine their enrollment eligibility.

Dishonorable and bad conduct discharges issued by general courts-martial may bar VA benefits. Veterans in prison and parolees must contact a VA regional office to determine eligibility. VA benefits will not be provided to any veteran or dependent wanted for an outstanding felony warrant.

The VA provides a Medical Benefits Package, a standard enhanced health benefits plan available to all enrolled veterans. This plan emphasizes preventive and primary care and offers a full range of outpatient and inpatient services within the VA health care system.

You may be eligible for VA benefits if you are:

- A veteran
- A veteran's dependent
- A surviving spouse, child, or parent of a deceased veteran
- An active duty military service member
- A member of the Reserve or National Guard

The VA maintains an annual enrollment system to manage the provision of quality hospital and outpatient medical care and treatment to all enrolled veterans. A priority system ensures that veterans with service-connected disabilities and those below the low-income threshold can be enrolled in VA's health care system. Enrolled veterans who are traveling or who spend time away from their primary treatment facility may obtain care at any VA health care facility across the country without having to reapply.

Enrolling for VA health care

For most veterans, entry into the VA health care system begins by applying for enrollment. To apply, complete VA Form 10-10EZ, Application for Health Benefits, which may be obtained from any VA health care facility or regional benefits office, or online at **www.1010ez.med.va.gov/sec/vha/1010ez**.

Those seeking a VA benefit for the first time must submit a copy of their service discharge form (DD-214, DD-215, or for WWII veterans, a WD form), which documents service dates and type of discharge, or give their full name, military service number, and branch and dates of service. The veteran's service discharge form should be kept in a safe location accessible to the veteran and next of kin or designated representative.

The number of veterans who can be enrolled in the health care program is determined by the amount of money Congress gives VA each year. Funds are limited, so the VA sets up priority groups to make sure certain groups of veterans can be enrolled before others.

Once you apply for enrollment, your eligibility will be verified. Based on your specific eligibility status, you will be assigned a priority group. The priority groups range from 1 to 8 with 1 being the highest priority for enrollment. Some veterans may have to agree to pay a copay to be placed in certain priority groups.

You may be eligible for more than one Enrollment Priority Group. In that case, VA will always place you in the highest priority group that you are eligible for. Under the Medical Benefits Package, the same services are generally available to all enrolled veterans.

Enrollment Priority Groups Definition	
1	• Veterans with VA-rated service-connected disabilities rated 50 percent or more • Veterans determined by VA to be unemployable due to service-connected conditions
2	• Veterans with VA-rated service-connected disabilities rated 30 to 40 percent • Veterans who are former prisoners of war (POWs)
3	• Veterans who are former prisoners of war (POWs) • Veterans awarded a Purple Heart medal • Veterans whose discharge was for a disability that was incurred or aggravated in the line of duty • Veterans with VA-rated service-connected disabilities rated 10 to 20 percent • Veterans awarded special eligibility classification under Title 38, U.S.C., § 1151, "benefits for individuals disabled by treatment or vocational rehabilitation" • Veterans awarded the Medal of Honor (MOH)
4	• Veterans who are receiving aid and attendance or housebound benefits from VA • Veterans who have been determined by VA to be catastrophically disabled

Enrollment Priority Groups Definition	
5	• Nonservice-connected veterans and noncompensable service-connected veterans rated 0 percent disabled by VA with annual income and/or net worth below the VA national income threshold and geographically-adjusted income threshold for their resident location • Veterans receiving VA pension benefits • Veterans eligible for Medicaid programs
6	• World War I veterans • Compensable 0 percent service-connected veterans • Veterans exposed to ionizing radiation during atmospheric testing or during the occupation of Hiroshima and Nagasaki • Project 112/SHAD participants • Veterans who served in the Republic of Vietnam between January 9,1962, and May 7, 1975 • Veterans of the Persian Gulf War that served between August 2, 1990 and November 11, 1998 • Veterans who served in a theater of combat operations after November 11, 1998, as follows: Currently enrolled veterans and new enrollees who were discharged from active duty on or after January 28, 2003, are eligible for the enhanced benefits for five years post discharge.
7	• Veterans with gross household income below the geographically adjusted income threshold (GMT) for their resident location. They agree to pay copays.
8	• Veterans with gross household income above the VA national income threshold and the geographically adjusted income threshold for their resident location. They agree to pay copays. **Veterans eligible for enrollment:** Noncompensable 0 percent service-connected and: Subpriority a: Enrolled as of January 16, 2003, and who have remained enrolled since that date and/or placed in this subpriority due to changed eligibility status Subpriority b: Enrolled on or after June 15, 2009, whose income exceeds the current VA National Income Thresholds or VA National Geographic Income Thresholds by 10 percent or less **Veterans eligible for enrollment:** Nonservice-connected and: Subpriority c: Enrolled as of January 16, 2003, and who have remained enrolled since that date and/or placed in this subpriority due to changed eligibility status Subpriority d: Enrolled on or after June 15, 2009, whose income exceeds the current VA National Income Thresholds or VA National Geographic Income Thresholds by 10 percent or less **Veterans not eligible for enrollment:** Veterans not meeting the criteria above: Subpriority e: Noncompensable 0 percent service-connected Subpriority g: Nonservice-connected

The priority groups are complicated and some reference financial thresholds.

The character of discharge you received from the military can be a factor. It is not an issue if you received:

* An honorable discharge
* A general discharge
* A discharge under honorable conditions

If you have a different character of discharge, you still may be eligible for care. Contact your enrollment coordinator at your local VA health care facility to see if you qualify.

The length of your service also may matter. It depends on when you served. There is no length of service requirement for:

- Former enlisted persons who started active duty before September 8, 1980
- Former officers who first entered active duty before October 17, 1981

All other veterans must have 24 months of continuous active duty military service.

However, you do not have to meet the 24 continuous months of active duty service requirement if you:

- Were a reservist who was called to active duty. You completed the term for which you were called and were granted an other than dishonorable discharge.

- Were a National Guard member who was called to active duty by federal executive order. You completed the term for which you were called were granted an other than dishonorable discharge

Veteran Privacy

Veterans enrolled in the VA health care system are afforded privacy rights under federal law. VA's Notice of Privacy Practices, which describes how VA may use and disclose veterans' medical information, is also available online at **www.va.gov/vhapublications/ViewPublication.asp?pub_ID=1089.**

Priority scheduling for service-connected veterans

VA will provide you priority access to care if you are a veteran who:

- Needs care of a service-connected disability or
- Are 50 percent service-connected or higher and need care for any condition.

In this case, VA will schedule you for a primary care evaluation within 30 days of desired date. If your outpatient appointment cannot be scheduled within this time, VA will arrange to have you seen within 30 days at another VA health care facility or obtain the services on fee basis, under a sharing agreement or contract at VA expense.

All other veterans will be scheduled for a primary care appointment as soon as one becomes available.

When you do not have to enroll

Generally, you must be enrolled in VA health care system to receive benefits offered in the Medical Benefits Package. However, certain veterans do not need to be enrolled to receive medical care benefits.

You do not have to be enrolled if you:

- You have been determined by VA to be 50 percent or more disabled from service-connected (SC) conditions.

- You are seeking care for a VA-rated service-connected disability only.

- It is less than one year since you were discharged for a disability that the military determined was incurred or aggravated by your service but that VA has not yet rated.

Veterans who are enrolled will remain enrolled without having to reapply for benefit annually. However, some veterans will need to update their financial information yearly to keep their enrollment priority current. VA will contact these veterans when it is time to update their financial information.

Combat veteran eligibility and special benefits

If you are a combat veteran, you might be eligible for special priority and consideration for VA health care benefits. The National Defense Authorization Act of 2008, signed into law on January 28, 2008, extended the period of eligibility for health care for veterans who served in combat operations after November 11, 1998.

Under the "combat veteran" authority, the VA provides cost-free health care services and nursing home care for conditions possibly related to military service and enrollment in Priority Group 6, unless eligible for enrollment in a higher priority group to combat veterans who were discharged or released from active service on or after January 28, 2003. These veterans are now eligible to enroll in the VA health care system for five years from the date of discharge or release. The five-year enrollment period applicable to these veterans begins on the discharge or separation date of the service member from active duty military service, or in the case of multiple call-ups, the most recent discharge date.

Combat veterans, while not required to disclose their income information, may do so to determine their eligibility for a higher priority status, beneficiary travel benefits, and exemption of copays for care unrelated to their military service.

The health care benefits available under the "combat veteran" authority include:

- Cost-free care and medications provided for conditions potentially related to combat service

- Enrollment in Priority Group 6 unless eligible for enrollment in a higher priority group
- Full access to VA's Medical Benefits Package

Veterans who enroll with VA under this authority will continue to be enrolled even after their enhanced eligibility period ends. At the end of their enhanced eligibility period, Veterans enrolled in Priority Group 6 may be shifted to Priority Group 7 or 8, depending on their income level, and might be required to make applicable copays.

For those veterans who do not enroll during their enhanced eligibility period, eligibility for enrollment and subsequent care is based on other factors, such as a compensable service-connected disability, VA pension status, catastrophic disability determination, or the veteran's financial circumstances. For this reason, combat veterans strongly are encouraged to apply for enrollment within their enhanced eligibility period, even if no medical care is currently needed.

Veterans who qualify under this special eligibility are not subject to copays for conditions potentially related to their combat service. However, unless otherwise exempted, combat veterans either must disclose their prior year gross household income or decline to provide their financial information and agree to make applicable copays for care or services VA determines are clearly unrelated to their military service.

Dental

Eligibility for VA dental benefits is based on specific guidelines and differs significantly from eligibility requirements for medical care. Combat Veterans may be authorized dental treatment as reasonably necessary for the one-time correction of dental conditions if:

- They served on active duty and were discharged or released from active duty under conditions other than dishonorable from a period of service not less than 90 days.

- The certificate of discharge or release does not bear a certification that the veteran was provided, within the 90-day period immediately before the date of such discharge or release, a complete dental examination (including dental X-rays) and all appropriate dental service and treatment indicated by the examination to be needed.

- Application for VA dental treatment is made within 180 days of discharge or release under conditions other than dishonorable.

Copay and Charges

There is no monthly premium required to use VA care. You may, however, have to agree to a copay.

Although many veterans qualify for cost-free health care services based on a compensable service-connected condition or other qualifying factor, most veterans are required to complete an annual financial assessment or means test to determine if they qualify. Veterans whose gross household income and net worth exceed the established threshold, and those who choose not to complete the financial assessment must agree to pay the required copays to become eligible for VA health care services. Note that new veterans who apply for enrollment after January 16, 2003, and who decline to provide income information are not eligible for enrollment. Along with their enrollment confirmation and priority group assignment, enrollees will receive information regarding their copay requirements, if applicable.

Who should provide a financial assessment (Means Test)?

VA is required to verify the gross household income (spouse and dependents, if any) of most non-service-connected or noncompensable 0 percent service-connected veterans to confirm the accuracy of their:

- Eligibility for VA health care
- Copay status
- Enrollment priority group assignment.

In determining your VA health care benefit, it is to your advantage to provide your income information if your gross household income (less allowable deductions) is equal to or less than the amount on the Financial Assessment Threshold Calculator. **www.va.gov/healthbenefits/resources/gmt/index. asp**. From the amounts you report on the Financial Worksheet during your enrollment at **www.1010ez.med.va.gov/sec/vha/1010ez**, VA will calculate and inform you of your income-based benefits.

Current year income and net worth can be considered when there is a hardship. VA verifies your gross household income (spouse and dependents, if any) by matching the financial data you provided with financial records maintained by IRS and SSA. If the matching process reveals that your gross household income is higher than the threshold, you will be provided an opportunity to review the IRS and SSA data and provide additional information regarding the difference. Veterans subject to this process are notified individually by mail and provided all related information.

At the end of the income verification process, if it is determined that your gross household income is higher than the threshold:

- Your priority group assignment will be changed.
- You will be required to pay copay.
- The facilities that provided you care will be notified to bill you for services provided during the period covered by your income assessment.
- You will be provided with your due process/appeal rights.

If you decline to give your financial information, the VA will:

- Place you in Priority Group 8
- Require you to agree to pay the copay fees for Group 8 before treatment can be given

Veterans applying for enrollment on or after January 17, 2003, who are assigned to Priority Group 8 are not eligible for enrollment or care of their non-service-connected conditions.

Many veterans qualify for cost-free health care and/or medications based on:

- Receiving a Purple Heart medal
- Former prisoner of war status
- Compensable service-connected disabilities
- Low income
- Other qualifying factors including treatment related to their military service experience

If you are now receiving VA compensation for a service-connected disability or VA pension benefits, your VA medical care and/or prescription copays may be reduced or eliminated. You also may be eligible for a refund of copay charges you have paid previously based on this decision. For further information, contact the enrollment coordinator at your local VA medical center.

Services exempt from copays

Some services veterans might need could be exempt from copays, no matter what your priority group or disability rating. The following services are always exempt for copays:

- Special registry examinations offered by VA to evaluate possible health risks associated with military service
- Counseling and care for military sexual trauma
- Compensation and pension examination requested by VBA
- Care that is part of a VA approved research project
- Care related to a VA-rated service connected disability
- Readjustment counseling and related mental health services for (PTSD)
- Emergency Treatment at other than VA facilities
- Care for cancer of head or neck caused from nose or throat radium treatments given while in the military
- Publicly announced VA public health initiatives (i.e. health fairs)
- Care related to service for veterans who served in combat or against a hostile force during a period of hostilities after November 11, 1998

- Laboratory services such as flat film radiology services and electrocardiograms
- Preventive screenings (hypertension, hepatitis C, tobacco, alcohol, colorectal cancer, etc.)
- Immunizations (such as influenza and pneumococcal)

Copays and health insurance

VA is required to bill private health insurance providers for medical care, supplies, and prescriptions provided for care veterans receive for their non-service connected conditions. Generally, VA cannot bill Medicare but can bill Medicare supplemental health insurance for covered services.

All veterans applying for VA medical care are required to provide information on their health insurance coverage, including coverage provided under policies of their spouses. Veterans are not responsible for paying any remaining balance of VA's insurance claim not paid or covered by their health insurance, and any payment received by VA may be used to offset a veteran's VA copay responsibility.

If you cannot afford to pay for the copay options, even with the help of your insurance company, there are three options:

1. Request a waiver of the copays you currently owe. To request a waiver, you must submit proof that you cannot afford financially to make payments to VA. Contact the revenue coordinator at the VA health care facility where you receive care for more information.

2. Request a hardship determination, so you will not be charged in the future. If you request a hardship, you are asking VA to change your priority group assignment to a lower number. You will need to submit current financial information, and a decision will be made based on the information you provide. Contact the enrollment coordinator at your local VA for more information.

3. Request a compromise. A compromise is an offer and acceptance of a partial payment in settlement and full satisfaction of the debt as it

exists at the time the offer is made. Most compromise offers that are accepted must be for a lump sum payment payable in full 30 days from the date of acceptance of the offer. Contact the enrollment coordinator at your local VA for more information.

Former Prisoners of War (POWs)

Since World War I, more than 142,000 Americans, including 85 women, have been captured and interned as POWs. Not included in this figure are nearly 93,000 Americans who were lost or never recovered. Only one-fifth of America's former POWs since World War I are still living (about 22,641). More than 90 percent of living former POWs were captured and interned during World War II. About 15,367 former POWs are in receipt of compensation for service-connected injuries, diseases, or illnesses.

In 1981, Congress passed Public Law 97-37, "Former Prisoners of War Benefit Act." This law accomplished several things. It established an Advisory Committee on Former Prisoners of War and mandated medical and dental care. It also identified certain diagnoses as presumptive service-connected conditions for former POWs. Subsequent public laws and policy decisions by the secretary of

veterans affairs have added additional diagnoses to the list of presumptive conditions. Refer to the chart above for the presumptive conditions associated with being a former POW.

Additionally, the VA health care system affords priority treatment for former POWs. Those who have a service-connected disability are eligible for VA health care. This includes hospital, nursing home, and outpatient treatment. Former POWs who do not have a service-connected disability are eligible for VA hospital and nursing home care — without regard to their ability to pay. They also are eligible for outpatient care on a priority basis second only to veterans with service-connected disabilities.

While former POWs are receiving treatment in an approved outpatient treatment program, they are eligible for needed medicines, glasses, hearing aids, or prostheses. They also are eligible for all needed dental care. There is no copayment requirement for former POWs at VA pharmacies.

Former POWs can apply for compensation for their service-connected injuries, diseases, or illnesses by completing VA Form 21-526, Veterans Application for Compensation and/or Pension. They also can apply online at **http://vabenefits.vba.va.gov/vonapp.**

Health Care Benefits

Once you are enrolled in the VA health care program, you will have access to a number of services and benefits offered by or paid for at least in part by the VA. This section will cover some of these benefits and services.

Preventive care

Some veterans think you only go to the doctor when something is wrong. Why go to the doctor when you feel healthy? Because an annual checkup may help you stay healthy longer.

An annual checkup can provide your physician with valuable information should you become ill. It also can help diagnose disease early and allows your doctor give you important advice on disease prevention. In order to keep you healthy and keep the severe treatments to a minimum, the VA's health benefits include important preventive care services for your use. At any VA facility, you may schedule:

- Periodic medical exams (including gender-specific exams)
- Health education, including nutrition education
- Immunization against infectious disease
- Counseling on inheritance of genetically determined disease

These procedures may or may not require a copay depending on your priority group and disability rating. Check with your local VA medical facility or online to find out what your options for preventative care are.

Mental health care

VA provides specialty inpatient and outpatient mental health services at its medical centers and community-based outpatient clinics. They provide cost-free military sexual trauma counseling and referral, including appropriate care and services, to overcome psychological trauma resulting from a physical assault or battery of a sexual nature or from sexual harassment that occurred while the veteran was on active duty or was on Active Duty for Training (ADUTRA).

Mental health services are available in specialty clinics, primary care clinics, nursing homes, and residential care facilities. Specialized programs, such as mental health intensive case management, day centers, work programs and psychosocial rehabilitation are provided for those with serious mental health problems.

The list of services and programs that Mental Health supports include:

- Inpatient care
- Residential care
- Outpatient mental health care
- Homeless programs
- Programs for incarcerated veterans
- Specialized PTSD services
- Military sexual trauma
- Psychosocial rehabilitation and recovery services
- Substance use disorders
- Suicide programs
- Geriatrics
- Violence prevention
- Evidence based psychotherapy programs
- Mental health disaster response/post deployment activities
- Suicide prevention

Dealing with PTSD

About one-third of these combat veterans who seek care from VA have a possible diagnosis of a mental disorder, and VA has significantly expanded its counseling and mental health services. VA has launched new programs, including dozens of new mental health teams based in VA medical centers focused on early identification and management of stress-related disorders, and the recruitment of about 100 combat veterans in its Readjustment Counseling Service to provide briefings to transitioning servicemen and women regarding military-related readjustment needs.

Many of the challenges facing the soldiers returning from Afghanistan and Iraq are stressors that have been identified and studied in veterans of previous wars. VA has developed world-class expertise in treating chronic mental health problems, including post-traumatic stress disorder (PTSD).

Post-traumatic stress involves a normal set of reactions to a trauma such as war. Sometimes it becomes a disorder with the passage of time when feelings or issues related to the trauma are not dealt with and are suppressed by the individual. This can result in problems readjusting to community life following the trauma. Since the war began, VA has activated dozens of new PTSD programs around the country to assist veterans in dealing with the emotional toll of combat. In addition, 207 readjustment counseling "vet centers" provide easy access in consumer-friendly facilities apart from traditional VA medical centers.

One early scientific study indicated the estimated risk for PTSD from service in the Iraq War was 18 percent, while the estimated risk for PTSD from the Afghanistan mission was 11 percent. Data from multiple sources now indicate that approximately 10 to 15 percent of soldiers develop PTSD after deployment to Iraq and another 10 percent have significant symptoms of PTSD, depression, or anxiety and may benefit from care. Alcohol misuse and relationship problems add to these rates. Combat veterans are at higher risk for psychiatric problems than military personnel serving in noncombat locations, and more frequent and more intensive combat is associated with higher risk. With military pre- and post-deployment health assessment programs seeking to destigmatize mental health treatment, coupled with simplified access to VA care for combat veterans after discharge, experts believe initial high rates likely will decrease.

Studies of PTSD patients have suggested as many as half may enjoy complete remission and the majority of the remainder will improve. Research has led to scientifically developed treatment guidelines covering a variety of modern therapies with which clinicians have had success. Treatments range from psychological first aid to cognitive behavioral therapy. More information about VA's PTSD programs is available at **www.ptsd.va.gov/public/pages/fslist-ptsd-overview.asp** and **www.ncptsd.va.gov**.

Bereavement counseling

VA health care facilities offer bereavement counseling to veterans and their family members who are receiving VA health care benefits. Bereavement counseling also is provided parents, spouses, and children of Armed Forces personnel who died in the service of their country. Also eligible are family members of reservists and National Guardsmen who die while on duty. Counseling is provided at Vet Centers. The nearest Vet Center locations can be found by going to **www.vetcenter.va.gov.**

Emergency care

A medical emergency generally is defined as a condition of such a nature that a prudent layperson would reasonably expect that delay in seeking immediate medical attention would be hazardous to life or health.

You may receive emergency care at a non-VA health care facility at VA expense when a VA facility (or other federal health care facility with which VA has an agreement) cannot furnish economical care due to your distance from the facility or when VA is unable to furnish the needed emergency services.

Service-connected conditions

VA may pay for your non-VA emergency care for a rated service-connected disability or for your nonservice-connected condition associated with and held to be aggravating your service-connected condition. They might cover any condition if you are an active participant in the VA Vocational Rehabilitation program, and you need treatment to make possible your entrance into a course of training or to prevent interruption of a course of training or other approved reason or any condition. They also might pay if you are rated as having a total disability permanent in nature resulting from your service-connected disability.

An emergency is deemed to have ended at the point when a VA provider has determined that, based on sound medical judgment, you should be transferred from the non-VA facility to a VA medical center.

Nonservice-connected conditions

VA may pay for emergency care provided in a non-VA facility for treatment of a nonservice-connected condition only if all of the following conditions are met:

- The episode of care cannot be paid under another VA authority.

- Based on an average knowledge of health and medicine (prudent layperson standard), you reasonably expected that delay in seeking immediate medical attention would have been hazardous to your life or health.

- A VA or other federal facility/provider was not feasibly available.

- You received VA medical care within a 24-month period preceding the non-VA emergency care.

- You are financially liable to the health care provider for the emergency care.

- The services were furnished by an emergency department or similar facility held out to provide emergency care to the public.

- You have no other coverage under a health plan (including Medicare, Medicaid and worker's compensation).

- You have no contractual or legal recourse against a third party that would, in whole, extinguish your liability.

Geriatrics and extended care

The mission of VA's Geriatrics and Extended Care is to advance quality care for aging and chronically ill veterans in the most efficient manner. VA provides assessments and care plan recommendations for the complex problems of aging.

Hospice services

The primary goal of hospice services is to provide comfort rather than cure for those with an advanced disease that is life-limiting. VA's interdisciplinary team of professionals and volunteers focuses on relief of suffering and maintenance of functional capacity as long as possible.

Respite care

Respite care is a program that provides short-term services to give the caregiver a period of relief from the demands of daily care for a chronically ill or disabled veteran.

Respite care services may include a short stay by the veteran in a VA Community Living Center (formerly known as VA nursing homes) or hospital; a short stay in a community nursing home; in-home services provided by a personal care aide; or services provided in an adult day health facility in the community. Respite care generally is limited to 30 days per year.

Domiciliary Residential Rehabilitation Treatment Program (DRRTP)

The mission of the Domiciliary Residential Rehabilitation Treatment Program (DRRTP — or Dom) is to provide an opportunity for motivated, at-risk veterans to participate in a residential, rehabilitative therapeutic community in order to assist the veteran in achieving his/her optimal level of functioning and to return to independent community living. The Dom is a short-term residential rehabilitation program where eligible veterans live and learn skills needed to live in the community and avoid a return to homelessness. Residents in the Domiciliary Care Program participate in a full range of rehabilitation services. This includes physical, behavioral, spiritual, psychosocial, addiction counseling, vocational, dietary, occupational therapy, and interventions.

In addition to the Dom programming, medical and mental health needs may be treated as needed by other staff (i.e. psychiatry, dental, PTSD team, women's clinic) during the resident's stay. The Dom does not provide shelter-type housing. Veterans in the program must be willing to participate in the treatment activities while they are living here.

While the amount of time varies for each resident, most veterans live at the domiciliary between one to six months depending on the programs and the veterans' individual needs. The DRRTP has three program tracks:

- Homeless prevention: Designed to help veterans regain psychosocial stability and learn the skills needed to prevent a return to homelessness. This is a 30- to 90-day track and may be combined with one of the other two tracks, depending on the veteran's needs.

- CWT (compensated work therapy): Designed to help veterans regain psychosocial stability, learn the skills needed to prevent a return to homelessness and return to competitive employment. This is a 30- to 120-day track and may be combined with one of the other two tracks, depending on the veteran's needs.

- Intensive substance abuse residential rehabilitation: This is a 30- to 60-day intensive residential admission focused primarily on recovery from addiction. Depending on the needs of the individual veteran, this may be combined with services in the homeless track (for veterans who do not plan to return to work) or CWT track (for veterans who have a reasonable expectation/desire to return to work). Programming for this track is integrated in the Alcohol and Drug Abuse Treatment Program (ADATP).

Adult day health care

Adult day health care is an outpatient day program consisting of health maintenance, rehabilitative services, socialization, and caregiver support. Veterans receiving adult day health care are often frail, elderly, and functionally impaired. Adult day health care includes key program elements to address health needs, physical and cognitive functions, and social support. The emphasis is on helping participants and their caregivers develop the knowledge and skills necessary to manage care at home.

Applying for long-term care

Non-service-connected and 0 percent service-connected enrolled veterans with income over the single pension rate will need to complete VA Form 10-10EC, Application for Extended Care Services in addition to a VA Form 10-10EZ available at **www.1010ez.med.va.gov/sec/vha/1010ez**.

Veterans with a compensable service-connected disability are exempt from long-term care copays.

Home health care

Home health care includes VA's Skilled Home Health Care Services (SHHC) and Homemaker and Home Health Aide Services (H/HHA).

SHHC services are in-home services provided by specially trained personnel, including nurses, physical therapists, occupational therapists, speech therapists, and social workers. Care includes clinical assessment, treatment planning and treatment provision, health status monitoring, patient and family education, reassessment, referral, and follow-up. H/HHA services are personal care and related support services that enable frail or disabled veterans to live at home.

Pharmacy / prescription benefits

Veterans enjoy free or low-cost prescriptions from VA facilities. VA's prescription benefit ensures that our veterans receive safe, effective, medically necessary medications that represent a good value. If a VA primary care provider is treating you, you will be provided all necessary medications for your treatment. Some veterans may receive their VA medications free of charge based on their service-connected disabilities, while those without service-connected disabilities are charged a copayment for each 30-day supply of medications VA provides.

There are several ways you can refill your prescriptions.

Online: You can now use the "My HealtheVet" website to refill your VA prescriptions and view your VA prescription history online. To access prescription refill, you must be a registered user of My HealtheVet. If you are not a registered user, to register and learn how to use prescription refill, visit the My HealtheVet website at **www.myhealth.va.gov**.

Mail Order: Medication refills can be requested by mailing the refill notice provided to you at the time of your original fill. Your order will be processed through the pharmacy mail-out program. Routine refills cannot be processed at the pharmacy windows (unless there are special circumstances).

Telephone: Some VA pharmacies have toll-free automated telephone refill systems. See the phone number listing for your local VA facility.

Filling prescriptions from non-VA providers

VA will provide medications that are prescribed by VA providers in conjunction with VA medical care. Medications are prescribed from an approved list of medications called a formulary. VA will fill prescriptions prescribed by a non-VA provider only if all of the following criteria are met:

- You are enrolled in VA health benefits.
- You have an assigned Primary Care Provider.
- Your have provided your VA health care provider with your medical records from your non-VA provider.
- Your VA health care provider agrees with the medication prescribed by your non-VA provider.

Your VA health care provider is under no obligation to prescribe a medication recommended by a non-VA provider.

Dental benefits

Dental benefits are provided by the Department of Veterans Affairs (VA) according to law.

In some instances, VA is authorized to provide extensive dental care, while in other cases treatment may be limited.

Outpatient care

The eligibility for outpatient dental care is not the same as for most other VA medical benefits and is categorized into classes. If you are eligible for VA dental care under Class I, IIC, or IV, you are eligible for any necessary dental care to maintain or restore oral health and masticatory function, including repeat care. Other classes have time and/or service limitations.

If you:	You are eligible for:	Through:
Have a service-connected compensable dental disability or condition	Any needed dental care	Class I
Are a former prisoner of war	Any needed dental care	Class IIC
Have service-connected dis- abilities rated 100% disabling, or are unemployable and paid at the 100% rate due to service connected conditions	Any needed dental care [Please note: Veterans paid at the 100% rate based on a temporary rating, such as extended hospitalization for a service-connected disability, convalescence or pre-stabilization are not eligible for comprehensive outpatient dental services based on this temporary rating.]	Class IV
Apply for dental care within 180 days of discharge or release (under conditions other than dishonorable) from a period of active duty of 90 days or more during the Persian Gulf War era	One-time dental care if your DD214 certificate of discharge does not indicate that a complete dental examination and all appropriate dental treatment had been rendered before discharge.	Class II
Have a service-connected non- compensable dental condition or disability resulting from combat wounds or service trauma	Needed care for the service-connected condition(s). A Dental Trauma Rating (VA Form 10-564-D) or VA Regional Office Rating Decision letter (VA Form 10-7131) identifies the tooth/ teeth eligible for care	Class IIA

If you:	You are eligible for:	Through:
Have a dental condition clinically determined by VA to be associated with and aggravating a service-connected medical condition	Dental care to treat the oral conditions that are determined by a VA dental professional to have a direct and material detrimental effect to your service-connected medical condition	Class III
Are actively engaged in a 38 USC vocational rehabilitation program	Dental care to the extent necessary as determined by a VA dental professional to: • Make possible your entrance into a rehabilitation program • Achieve the goals of your vocational rehabilitation program • Prevent interruption of your rehabilitation program • Hasten the return to a rehabilitation program if you are in interrupted or leave status • Hasten the return to a rehabilitation program of a Veteran placed in discontinued status because of illness, injury or a dental condition • Secure and adjust to employment during the period of employment assistance, or enable you to achieve maximum independence in daily living	Class V
Are receiving VA care or are scheduled for inpatient care and require dental care for a condition complicating a medical condition currently under treatment	Dental care to treat the oral conditions that are determined by a VA dental professional to complicate your medical condition currently under treatment	Class VI
Are an enrolled veteran who may be homeless and receiving care under VHA Directive 2007-039	A one-time course of dental care that is determined medically necessary to relieve pain, assist you to gain employment, or treat moderate, severe, or complicated and severe gingival and periodontal conditions	Class IIB

- Note: Public Law 83 enacted June 16, 1955, amended Veterans' eligibility for outpatient dental services. As a result, any veteran who received a dental award letter from VBA dated before 1955 in which VBA determined the dental conditions to be noncompensable are no longer eligible for Class II outpatient dental treatment.

Inpatient program

Veterans receiving hospital, nursing home, or domiciliary care will be provided dental services that are professionally determined by a VA dentist, in consultation with the referring physician, to be essential to the management of the patient's medical condition under active treatment.

For more information about eligibility for VA medical and dental benefits, contact VA at 877-222-VETS (8387) or **www.va.gov/healtheligibility**.

Eyeglasses and hearing aids

A large number of vets are eligible to receive hearing aids and eyeglasses through a VA medical center. Those eligible must meet at least one of the following requirements:

- Must have a compensable service-connected disability
- Must have been a former POW
- Must have received a Purple Heart service award
- Must be receiving benefits
- Must be in receipt of an increased pension because they are homebound and require regular assistance
- Those who have vision or hearing loss or impairment connected to diseases and chronic medical conditions for which the vet is receiving care at a VA medical center or a condition that occurred following treatment for another illness, i.e. stroke, brain injury, etc.
- Those with evident functional or cognitive issues that affect the veteran's ability to perform daily tasks
- Those who have vision or hearing impairments so significant that they interfere with their daily lives, including participation in medical treatment
- Those who have service-connected vision disabilities rated zero percent or service-connected hearing issues rated zero percent

For veterans who are interested in learning more about their eligibility, the first step is to verify your enrollment in the VA Health Care Network. Enrollment permits the vet to receive both inpatient and outpatient services ranging from immunizations to surgery to mental health services.

Otherwise, hearing aids and eyeglasses will be provided only in special circumstances as specified by the VA and not for normally occurring hearing or vision loss.

Foreign medical program

The Foreign Medical Program (FMP) is a program for veterans who live or travel overseas. Under the FMP, the VA will pay the allowable amount for treatment of a service-connected disability or medical services needed as part of a VA vocational rehabilitation program.

The VA's Health Administration Center (HAC), located in Denver, Colorado, handles the FMP program for medical services provided to eligible veterans in all foreign countries except the Philippines. For more information, contact the HAC toll free at 877-345-8179 or visit their website at **www.va.gov/hac/forbeneficiaries/fmp/fmp.asp**.

How to find the Veterans Administration Facility Near You

VA facilities listing and telephone numbers can be found on the Internet at **www2.va.gov/directory/guide/home.asp** or in the local telephone directory under the "U.S. Government" listings. Veterans also can visit the VA health eligibility website at **www.va.gov/healtheligibility** or call VA toll-free at 877-222-VETS (8387).

MyHealthEVet

To keep up to speed with the modern technologies, the VA has established a website for veterans that lets them manage their health care and find out more about their eligibility for benefits. It is called MyHealthEVet (MHV). This site is located at **www.myhealth.va.gov**.

MHV registrants will be able to view appointments, copay balances, and key portions of their VA medical records online. MHV provides access to:

- Trusted health information
- Links to federal and VA benefits and resources
- The Personal Health Journal
- Online VA prescription refill

The Personal Health Journal provides valuable features for managing and tracking your personal health information, including the following options:

- Contact information
- Emergency contacts
- Health care providers
- Treatment locations
- Health insurance information

The Personal Health Journal will also help you design your wallet ID card, a handy, preformatted wallet card with all of your medical information for convenient reference. It also has open spaces for you to list allergies and other critical medical conditions. You also will be able to record important events from your military service, exposures you think you may have experienced, and assignments related to your health history.

MHV offers each veteran access to his or her saved medications, over-the-counter drugs, herbals, and supplements. You can record the name, starting and ending date, prescription number, and dosage. You also can keep track of your allergies by date, severity, reaction, diagnosis, and comments.

Keep track of your tests by test name, date of test, location test was performed, provider's name, results, and any comments. Monitor illnesses, accidents or other events by logging their date, treatment prescribed or comments regarding the event. Record the immunization, date received, method used, and any reactions you might have.

Another useful function is the Health eLogs. Users are able to track their readings for many health aspects including:

- Blood pressure
- Blood sugar
- Cholesterol
- Body temperature
- Body weight
- Heart rate
- Pain

You may sign up for MyHealthEVet at **www.myhealth.va.gov/index.html**.

Beneficiary travel benefits

If you meet the criteria below, you may be eligible for mileage reimbursement or special mode transport in association with obtaining VA health care services.

You qualify if:

- You have a service-connected (SC) rating of 30 percent or more.
- You are traveling for treatment of a SC condition.
- You receive a VA pension.
- Your income does not exceed the maximum annual VA pension rate.
- You are traveling for a scheduled compensation or pension examination.

You qualify for special mode transportation (ambulance, wheelchair, van, etc.) if:

- Your medical condition requires an ambulance or a specially equipped van as determined by a VA clinician.
- You meet one of the eligibility criteria above.
- The travel is pre-authorized (authorization is not required for emergencies if a delay would be hazardous to life or health).

In order to reach a VA facility, you might need to travel. If you meet the requirements listed above, you could be eligible to be reimbursed for your mileage to the VA facility. For general travel, the VA will reimburse you

$0.415 (41.5 cents) per mile. Scheduled appointments qualify for round-trip mileage. Unscheduled visits may be limited to return mileage only.

Effective January 2009, there will be a deductible to reach before you will be reimbursed for your mileage. This deductible is $3 one-way ($6 round-trip). Deductible requirement is subject to a monthly cap of $18. Upon reaching $18 in deductibles or six one-way (three round-) trips, whichever comes first, travel payments made for the balance of that particular month will be free of deductible charges

A waiver of the deductible will be provided if you are eligible for travel and you:

- Are in receipt of a VA pension
- Are a NSC veteran and your previous year's income does not exceed, or your projected current calendar year's income, in the year of application will not exceed the applicable VA pension rate
- Are a SC veteran and your previous year's income does not exceed, or your projected current calendar year's income, in the year of application will not exceed the applicable national means test income threshold
- Are traveling for a scheduled compensation and pension exam

Health Benefits for Family Members of Veterans

Under certain circumstances, family members of veterans are eligible for health benefits. Some of the programs offered include the Civilian Health and Medical Program of the Department of Veterans Affairs (CHAMP-VA), Spina Bifida (SB), Children of Women Vietnam Veterans (CWVV), and Caregiver. Using these programs may reduce or eliminate your cost for medical supplies, office visits, or prescriptions. *CHAMPVA is covered in more detail in Chapter 6.*

Spina Bifida Health Care Program

The Spina Bifida Health Care Program is a health benefit program administered by the Department of Veterans Affairs for Vietnam and certain Korean veterans' birth children who have been diagnosed with spina bifida (except spina bifida occulta). The program provides reimbursement for medical services and supplies.

Children of Women Vietnam Veterans (CWVV) Program

The CWVV Health Care Program is a federal health benefits program for children with certain birth defects born to women Vietnam veterans. The CWVV Program is a fee for service (indemnity plan) program. The CWVV Program provides reimbursement for medical care-related conditions associated with certain birth defects except spina bifida, which is covered under the VA's Spina Bifida Health Care Program.

Children whose biological mother is a Vietnam veteran, who were conceived after the date on which the veteran entered the Republic of Vietnam, during the period beginning on February 28, 1961, and ending May 7, 1975, and who have one of the covered birth defects, as determined by the Veterans Benefits Administration (VBA) are eligible for the program.

Caregiver

Primary caregivers of OEF/OIF veterans may be eligible to receive a stipend and access to health care coverage if they already are not entitled to care or services under a health plan contract, including Medicare, Medicaid, or worker's compensation. Mental health counseling, including marriage and family counseling, also will be provided. Caregivers also may be eligible for travel, lodging, and per diem when they accompany the veteran for care or attend training.

The VA believes that caring and supporting family caregivers improves the lives of veterans. Learn more about how the VA supports family caregivers at **www.caregiver.va.gov**.

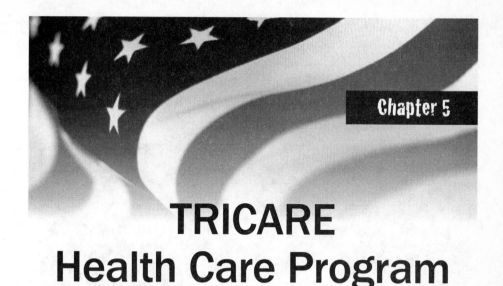

Chapter 5

TRICARE
Health Care Program

ctive duty military members are thoroughly familiar with TRI-
CARE benefits and TRICARE retiree dental benefits. Fewer
know that these benefits can extend past your active career and
into your retirement from the military. There are a variety of TRICARE,
dental, and other medical insurance options when you are retired or disabled. TRICARE and dental options are entitlements; however, they are
not free. Ultimately, you must weigh your insurance options to determine
if it is worth participating in either program.

What is TRICARE?

TRICARE is the health care program serving active duty service members,
retirees, their families, survivors, and certain former spouses worldwide. As
a major component of the Military Health System, TRICARE brings together the health care resources of the uniformed services and supplements
them with networks of civilian health care professionals, institutions, phar-

macies, and suppliers to provide access to high-quality health care services while maintaining the capability to support military operations.

To be eligible for TRICARE benefits, you must be registered in the Defense Enrollment Eligibility Reporting System. TRICARE offers several health plan options to meet the needs of its beneficiary population.

TRICARE eligibility

TRICARE is available to active duty service members and retirees of the seven uniformed services, their family members, survivors, and others who are registered in the Defense Enrollment Eligibility Reporting System (DEERS). In addition to your enrollment in DEERS, you must have a valid uniformed services identification card showing you are eligible for TRICARE.

TRICARE is available worldwide and is managed in four separate regions: three in the United States and one overseas region that is divided into three main areas.

The three regions in the United States include:

- TRICARE North
- TRICARE South
- TRICARE West

The overseas region includes:

- TRICARE Europe
- TRICARE Latin America and Canada
- TRICARE Pacific

TRICARE Prime

TRICARE Prime is a managed care option offering the most affordable and comprehensive coverage. TRICARE Prime is available in areas near military treatment facilities and where regional contractors have established TRICARE Prime networks.

Key features of TRICARE Prime include:

- Enrollment required to participate, but there are no enrollment fees for active duty service members and their families.
- Flexible enrollment options:
  o Online via the Beneficiary Web Enrollment website
  o Submit a TRICARE Prime Enrollment and PCM Change Form through the mail
  o Submit a TRICARE Prime Enrollment and PCM Change Form at a TRICARE Service Center
- Fewer out-of-pocket costs than other TRICARE options
- Enhanced coverage for vision and clinical preventive services
- Priority access for care at military treatment facilities
- Most care is received from an assigned primary care manager (PCM).
- Your PCM refers you to specialists when necessary.

- Point of service option available (to all but active duty service members) to receive care without requesting a referral from your PCM (resulting in higher out-of-pocket costs)
- No claims to file (in most cases)
- Easy to transfer enrollment when moving to another location in your TRICARE region or to a new TRICARE region
- Time and distance access standards for care, including wait times for urgent, routine, and specialty care

When you enroll in TRICARE Prime, you have an assigned primary care manager (PCM), either at a military treatment facility (MTF) or from the TRICARE network, who provides most of your care. Your PCM will refer you to a specialist for care he or she cannot provide and coordinate with your regional contractor for authorization, find a specialist in the network, and file claims on your behalf.

You have certain time and distance standards for care including wait times for urgent, routine, and specialty care. Other benefits include enhanced vision and preventive services and travel reimbursement for some specialty care.

TRICARE Prime eligibility

TRICARE Prime is available to the following beneficiaries as long as they are not entitled to Medicare Part A and Part B due to age (65):

- Active duty service members and their families
- Retired service members and their families
- Eligible former spouses
- Survivors
- National Guard and Reserve members and their families when the National Guard or Reserve member is activated for more than 30 consecutive days
- Retired National Guard and Reserve members and their families
- Medal of Honor recipients and their families

All eligible beneficiaries must live in a Prime Service Area (PSA). A PSA is a geographic area where TRICARE Prime benefits are offered. It is typically a geographic area around a military treatment facility and specific areas with a significant concentration of uniformed services personnel and retirees and their families. A PSA also must have a substantial medical community to support TRICARE Prime beneficiaries. If you do not live in a PSA, you may be eligible for TRICARE Prime Remote, or you may use TRICARE Standard and Extra.

It is important to note that, currently, discharged veterans have entitlements under CHAMPVA if disabled, or possibly through other programs if they served in the Gulf War, Iraq, or Afghanistan. *CHAMPVA will be discussed in the next chapter.*

Travel reimbursement

Non-active duty TRICARE Prime beneficiaries and TRICARE Prime Remote family members may qualify to have "reasonable travel expenses" reimbursed by TRICARE when they are referred by their primary care manager (PCM) for medically necessary, nonemergency specialty care at a location more than 100 miles (one way) from their PCM's office. Reasonable travel expenses are the actual costs incurred while traveling, including meals, gas, tolls, parking, and tickets for public transportation (i.e., airplane, train, bus, etc.).

Beneficiaries who may qualify for this travel reimbursement include:

- TRICARE Prime-enrolled active duty family members, including family members of activated National Guard or Reserve members
- TRICARE Prime-enrolled retired service members and their family members
- TRICARE Prime-enrolled transitional survivors, survivors, and former spouses
- Others enrolled in TRICARE Prime except for active duty service members

- TRICARE Prime Remote-enrolled active duty family members, including family members of activated National Guard or Reserve members
- TRICARE Prime Remote-enrolled transitional survivors

US Family Health Plan

The US Family Health Plan is an additional TRICARE Prime option available through networks of community-based, not-for-profit health care systems in six areas of the United States. You must live in the one of the designated US Family Health Plan service areas to enroll. The US Family Health Plan is the only TRICARE Prime program that offers benefits to beneficiaries age 65 and over, regardless of whether or not they have Medicare Part B.

Designated US Family Health Plan Providers	
Johns Hopkins Medicine *Serving Maryland; Washington D.C.; and parts of Pennsylvania, Virginia, Delaware, and West Virginia* **www.hopkinsmedicine.org**	**St. Vincent Catholic Medical Centers** *Serving New York City, Long Island, southern Connecticut, New Jersey, Philadelphia, and area suburbs* **www.svcmc.org**
Martin's Point Health Care *Serving Maine, New Hampshire, Vermont, upstate and western New York, and the northern tier of Pennsylvania* **www.martinspoint.org**	**CHRISTUS Health** *Serving southeast Texas and southwest Louisiana* **www.christushealth.org**
Brighton Marine Health Center *Serving Massachusetts, including Cape Cod; Rhode Island; and northern Connecticut* **http://brimarine.org**	**Pacific Medical Centers** *Serving the Puget Sound area of Washington state* **www.pacificmedicalcenters.org**

When you enroll in the US Family Health Plan, you will not access Medicare providers, military treatment facilities, or TRICARE network providers but instead receive your care (including prescription drug coverage) from a primary care physician that you select from a network of private physicians affiliated with one of the not-for-profit health care systems offering the plan. Your primary care physician assists you in getting appointments with specialists in the area and coordinates your care.

Active duty family members pay no enrollment fees and no out-of-pocket costs for any type of care as long as care is received from the US Family Health Plan provider. All other beneficiaries pay annual enrollment fees and network copayments.

Type of Care	Copayment
Outpatient	$12 per visit
Inpatient	$11 per day ($25 minimum charge)

If you live in one of the six designated areas, you may want to consider the US Family Health Plan. It is a robust Prime option that even offers enhanced coverage at each location. Visit **www.usfhp.com** for more information.

You may enroll in US Family Health Plan at any time during the year by completing an application for the plan in your area. Select your US Family Health Plan from the list above to download the correct enrollment application.

If Your Sponsor Dies

If you die after retiring from active duty, it is comforting to know that TRICARE continues to provide coverage for your family.

Widowed spouses remain eligible for TRICARE unless they remarry.

Children (biological or adopted) remain eligible up to the normal age limits. Your surviving family members may remain enrolled in TRICARE Prime but must arrange to pay the TRICARE Prime enrollment fee. TRICARE Standard and Extra cover family members who decide not to stay enrolled in TRICARE Prime.

TRICARE Standard and Extra

TRICARE Standard and Extra is a fee-for-service plan available to all non-active duty beneficiaries in the United States. Enrollment is not required.

Coverage is automatic as long as your information is current in the Defense Enrollment Eligibility Reporting System.

When using TRICARE Standard and Extra, you may visit any TRICARE-authorized provider, network or nonnetwork. Care at military treatment facilities is on a space-available basis only. You do not need a referral for any type of care, but some services might require prior authorization.

The type of provider you see determines which option you are using and how much you will pay out-of-pocket. If you visit a nonnetwork provider, you are using the Standard option. If you visit a network provider, you are using the Extra option. If using the Extra option, you will pay less out of pocket, and the provider will file claims for you.

Costs also vary depending on your military status (active duty family members versus retirees, their families and others). After you have met an annual deductible, you are responsible for paying a cost share (or percentage).

Beneficiary Category	Outpatient Cost Share	Inpatient Cost Share
Active duty family members	**Network Providers:** 15% of the negotiated rate **Nonnetwork Providers:** 20% of the TRICARE allowable charge	$16.85 per day ($25 minimum charge)
Retired service members and their families	**Network Providers:** 20% of the negotiated rate **Nonnetwork Providers:** 25% of the TRICARE allowable charge	**Nonnetwork facilities:** $535 per day or 25% for institutional services, whichever is less, plus 25% for separately billed professional charges **Network facilities:** $250 per day or 25% for institutional services, whichever is less, plus 20% for separately billed professional charges

TRICARE Standard Overseas

TRICARE Standard Overseas provides comprehensive coverage to active duty family members, retired service members and their families, and all others who do not or cannot enroll in TRICARE Prime Overseas. TRICARE Extra is not available in overseas locations. Enrollment is not required; coverage is automatic as long as your information is current in the Defense Enrollment Eligibility Reporting System.

When using TRICARE Standard Overseas, you will receive care from host-nation providers. You may seek care at a military treatment facility on a space-available basis only. You do not need a referral for any type of care, but some services might require prior authorization. You might have to pay the provider in full when you receive care and file a claim with TRICARE for reimbursement.

Costs vary depending on the sponsor's military status (active duty family members versus retirees, their families and others). After you have met an annual deductible, you are responsible for paying a cost share.

Beneficiary Category	Outpatient Cost Share	Inpatient Cost Share
Active duty family members	20% of the TRICARE allowable charge	Per diem charge ($25 minimum charge)
Retired service members and their families	25% of the TRICARE allowable charge	25% of billed charges for institutional services, plus 25 percent of covered costs for separately billed professional services

International SOS is the TRICARE Overseas Program contractor and will provide the assistance you need for claims, finding a provider, authorization, and much more.

TRICARE Reserve Select

TRICARE Reserve Select (TRS) is a premium-based health plan that qualified National Guard and Reserve members may purchase. TRS, which requires a monthly premium, offers coverage similar to TRICARE Standard and Extra.

Key features of TRS include:

• Available worldwide to most Selected Reserve members (and families) when not on active duty orders or covered under the Transitional Assistance Management Program

- Must qualify for and purchase TRS to participate
- Must pay monthly premiums. Failure to pay monthly premiums on time may result in disenrollment and an enrollment lockout.
- Freedom to manage your own health care; no assigned primary care manager
- Visit any TRICARE-authorized provider or qualified host nation provider (if located overseas)
- Pay fewer out-of-pocket costs when choosing a provider in the TRICARE network
- Network providers not available overseas
- No referrals are required, but some care may require prior authorization.
- May have to pay for services when they are received and then seek reimbursement
- May have to submit health care claims
- May receive care in a military treatment facility (MTF) on a space-available basis only
- Offers comprehensive health care coverage including TRICARE's prescription drug coverage

TRICARE Prime and TRICARE Standard for Retirees

Your TRICARE health benefits will change when you retire. Here is a quick look at how TRICARE changes:

Health care options

While on active duty, you must enroll in a TRICARE Prime option. Once you retire, you and your family can use any of the following health care options:

- TRICARE Prime (You must re-enroll and pay annual enrollment fees.)
- TRICARE Standard and Extra
- US Family Health Plan (in specific U.S. locations)

- TRICARE For Life (with Medicare Part A & B coverage)
- TRICARE Standard Overseas

Covered services

TRICARE will continue to provide comprehensive coverage to you and your family, including prescription drug coverage.

However, some services no longer will be covered:

- Eye exams are only covered if you re-enroll in TRICARE Prime
- Hearing aids
- TRICARE Extended Care Health Option services for family members
- Chiropractic care
- Dental care is now available through the TRICARE Retiree Dental Program
- Costs

While on active duty, you paid nothing out of pocket, and your family's costs were minimal. Now, as a retiree, you will see an increase in costs:

- Annual TRICARE Prime enrollment fees ($230/individual or $460 per family)
- TRICARE Prime network copayments
- TRICARE Standard and Extra costs increase by 5 percent
- Catastrophic cap increases from $1,000 to $3,000 annually per family
- No change in prescription costs
- Medicare-eligible family members must have Medicare Part B coverage to remain eligible when you retire.

TRICARE For Life for Medicare Users

TRICARE For Life (TFL) is TRICARE's Medicare-wraparound coverage available to all Medicare-eligible TRICARE beneficiaries, regardless of age or place of residence, provided they have Medicare Parts A and B.

What is Medicare/Medicaid?

Medicare is a health insurance program managed by the Centers for Medicare & Medicaid Services for:

- People age 65 or older
- People under age 65 with certain disabilities
- People with end-stage renal disease (ESRD)

Medicare Part A is hospital insurance. Medicare Part B is medical insurance. Under federal law, if you are a TRICARE beneficiary eligible for premium-free Medicare Part A because of a disability or ESRD, or are eligible based on turning age 65, you must have Medicare Part B coverage to remain TRICARE-eligible. The only exceptions are if you have a sponsor on active duty.

If you are an active duty family member eligible for or entitled to premium-free Medicare Part A, you do not have to have Medicare Part B until your sponsor retires to keep your TRICARE benefits. You may enroll in Part B during a Special Enrollment Period. The Special Enrollment Period is available to you anytime your sponsor is on active duty or within the first eight months of your sponsor's retirement. If you enroll in Part B after your sponsor's retirement date, you will have a break in TRICARE coverage. To avoid this break, enroll in Part B before your sponsor's retirement date.

If you do not enroll during the Special Enrollment Period, your next opportunity to enroll in Part B is during the General Enrollment Period, which occurs each year January 1 through March 31. Your Part B coverage will start on July 1, which means your TRICARE coverage will not be effective until July 1. You also may be required to pay the 10 percent Medicare surcharge for each 12-month period you were eligible to enroll in Part B, but did not.

If you are eligible for or entitled to premium-free Medicare Part A and enrolled in the US Family Health Plan (available in six locations), you do not have to have Medicare Part B for US Family Health Plan coverage. However, the Department of Defense (DOD) strongly encourages enrollment in Part B when you are first eligible. If you withdraw your enrollment from the US Family Health Plan or move to a non-US Family Health Plan area, you will not be eligible for other

TRICARE programs if you do not have Part B. If you do not enroll in Part B when first eligible, you may be required to pay the 10 percent Medicare surcharge for each 12-month period you were eligible to enroll in Part B, but did not.

TRICARE Reserve Select Members

If you are eligible for or entitled to premium-free Medicare Part A and enrolled in TRICARE Reserve Select (TRS), you do not have to have Medicare Part B, but the DOD strongly encourages enrollment in Part B when first eligible. Although TRICARE treats you as an active duty family member while in TRS, Medicare does not consider your sponsor to be actively employed by the military.

Disability. You are eligible for Medicare Part A (premium-free) and Part B (with a monthly premium) beginning the 25th month of receiving Social Security disability payments. The Social Security Administration (SSA) notifies you of your Medicare entitlement start date. If your disability claim and Medicare entitlement are awarded retroactively, it is important to make sure your Medicare Part A and Part B effective dates match. If your Medicare effective dates do not match, TRICARE can and will recoup payments made for claims paid when you had Part A coverage and no Part B.

Your Medicare entitlement continues up to four and a half years after your disability payments end. During this period, you still are required to have Part B to remain TRICARE-eligible.

End Stage Renal Disease. Medicare coverage is not automatic for people with ESRD. You need to file an application to receive Medicare benefits. Failure to file for Medicare benefits will result in loss of TRICARE coverage. Your Medicare coverage begins:

- The fourth month you are on renal dialysis
- The month you are admitted to a Medicare-approved hospital for kidney transplant, or in the following two months
- Two months before your transplant if your transplant is delayed more than two months after admission to the hospital

Age. The age for full Social Security payments gradually is increasing from 65 to 67. The age for Medicare eligibility is not changing; It continues to be 65.

- You become eligible for premium-free Medicare Part A at age 65 if you or your spouse paid into Social Security for at least 40 quarters (at least ten years of work). Failure to file for Medicare benefits results in loss of TRICARE coverage.

- If you already receive benefits from Social Security, the Railroad Retirement Board (RRB), or Office of Personnel Management, you automatically receive Medicare Part A and are enrolled in Medicare Part B starting the first day of the month you turn 65. If your birthday is on the first of the month, Part A is effective on the first day of the previous month.

- If you have not filed for Social Security benefits, RRB benefits, or a federal annuity from the Office of Personnel Management, you must file an application for Part A and Part B. To avoid the Medicare surcharge for late enrollment, you must enroll in Part B during your Medicare Initial Enrollment Period (IEP) (seven-month period that begins three months before you turn 65, or four months if your birthday is on the first of the month). To avoid a break in TRICARE coverage, be sure to enroll during the three to four months before you turn 65. If you wait until you are 65 or enroll during the last three months of your IEP, your Part B effective date and TRICARE coverage will be delayed.

Medicare's prescription drug coverage, Medicare Part D, is available to anyone who is eligible for Medicare (Part A or Part B). Beneficiaries who live overseas or who are in prison are not eligible for Medicare Part D.

You do not need to enroll in a Medicare Part D prescription drug plan to keep your TRICARE benefits. If you decide to enroll in a Medicare Part D prescription drug plan outside of your initial enrollment period, you will not be required to pay the Medicare Part D late enrollment penalty because TRICARE prescription drug coverage is creditable coverage.

Although Medicare is your primary insurance, TRICARE acts as your secondary payer to minimize your out-of-pocket expenses. TRICARE benefits include covering Medicare's coinsurance and deductible.

If you use a Medicare participating or nonparticipating provider, he or she will file your claims with Medicare. Medicare pays its portion and electronically forwards the claim to the TFL claims processor. TFL pays the provider directly for TRICARE-covered services. For services covered by both Medicare and TRICARE, Medicare pays first, and TFL pays your remaining coinsurance for TRICARE-covered services.

When using TFL, you do not pay any enrollment fees, but you must pay Medicare Part B monthly premiums. Your Part B premium is based on your income. For more information about Part B premiums visit **www. medicare.gov**.

Using TRICARE For Life overseas

Medicare provides coverage in the United States and U.S. Territories. When using TRICARE For Life in all other overseas locations, TRICARE is the primary payer, and you are responsible for paying TRICARE's annual deductible and cost shares. TRICARE beneficiaries who live overseas and who are eligible for premium-free Medicare Part A must have Part B to remain eligible for TRICARE even though Medicare does not provide coverage overseas.

International SOS is the TRICARE Overseas Program contractor and will provide the assistance you need for claims, finding a provider, medical information, and assistance and authorization for care.

TRICARE Retiree Dental Program

The TRICARE Retiree Dental Program, or TRDP, has been the premier dental plan since it was created by Congress and made available to Uniformed Services retirees and their family members on February 1, 1998. This program offers:

- Comprehensive coverage for the most commonly needed and sought-after dental services, including dental accidents and composite fillings on back teeth, immediately upon the coverage effective date

- The full scope of major benefits such as crowns, bridges, dentures, dental implant services, and orthodontics available after 12 months

- Coverage for dental emergencies when traveling outside the Enhanced TRDP service area described below

- Optimum cost savings and program value by giving enrollees the option to choose from an expansive list of participating network dentists in more than 150,000 locations nationwide who have agreed to provide treatment to TRDP enrollees at significantly reduced fees. (Enrollees also may choose any licensed dentist within the service area who is not in the TRDP network, but the dentist fees may be higher.)

- A new, expanded list of dentists for enrollees living and traveling overseas

- Affordable monthly premiums, low deductibles, and generous maximum allowances, including a lifetime orthodontic maximum of $1,500 per person

Service area

The TRDP offers covered services worldwide, with benefits based on whether you are enrolled in the Enhanced TRDP or the Enhanced-Overseas TRDP. The service area for enrollees in the Enhanced TRDP includes the United States, the District of Columbia, Puerto Rico, Guam, the U.S. Virgin Islands, American Samoa, the Commonwealth of the Northern Mariana Islands, and Canada. When traveling outside this service area, enrollees in the Enhanced TRDP are eligible for emergency dental services only; however, dependents of Enhanced TRDP enrollees who are full-time students studying overseas are eligible for the full scope of services, with verification of their overseas student status.

Coverage under the Enhanced-Overseas TRDP, which matches the scope of coverage described in the chart below, is available to enrollees who reside outside the Enhanced TRDP service area noted above. Upon their enrollment in the Enhanced-Overseas Program, enrollees receive a supplemental guide with details on the provisions that apply specifically to their overseas coverage.

Eligibility

You are eligible to enroll in the TRDP if you are:

- A member of the Uniformed Services who is entitled to Uniformed Services retired pay, even if you are 65 or older

- A member of the retired National Guard/Reserve, including those in the "gray-area" who are entitled to retired pay but will not begin receiving it until age 60

- A current spouse of an enrolled member

- A child of an enrolled member, up to age 21 or to age 23 if a full-time student (proof of full-time student status required), or older if disabled before losing eligibility

- An unremarried surviving spouse or eligible child of a deceased member who died while in retired status or while on active duty

- A Medal of Honor recipient and eligible family members, or an unremarried surviving spouse/eligible family members of a deceased recipient

- A current spouse and/or eligible child of a non-enrolled member with documented proof the non-enrolled member is: (a) eligible to receive ongoing comprehensive dental care from the Department of Veterans Affairs; (b) enrolled in a dental plan through employment and the plan is not available to family members; or (c) unable to obtain benefits through the TRDP due to a current and enduring medical or dental condition. Written documentation supporting any of these three situations must be submitted with your enrollment application.

- Former spouses and remarried surviving spouses are not eligible at this time.

This chart provides an overview of coverage under the Enhanced TRI-CARE Retiree Dental Program.

Benefits available during the first 12 months of enrollment:	*Delta Dental Pays:
Diagnostic services (such as exams)	100%
Preventive services (such as cleanings)	100%
Basic restorative services (such as fillings, including tooth-colored fillings on back teeth)	80%
Endodontics (such as root canals)	60%
Periodontics (such as gum treatment)	60%
Oral surgery (such as extractions)	60%
Emergency (such as treatment for minor pain)	80%
Dental accident coverage	100%
Additional services available after 12 months of continuous enrollment or if enrolled within four months after retirement:	
Cast crowns, onlays, and bridges	50%
Partial/full dentures	50%
Dental implant services	50%
Orthodontics	50%
Deductibles & Maximums	
Annual deductible (per person, $150 cap per family per benefit year)	$50
Annual maximum (per person per benefit year)	$1200
Orthodontic maximum (per person per lifetime)	$1500
Dental Accident Maximum (per person, per benefit year)	$1000
Benefit Year: October 1- September 30	

*The percentage paid is based on the allowed amount for each procedure. Although the coverage percentage is the same for all TRDP patients, total out-of-pocket costs may be higher if care is received from a non-network or overseas dentist. Covered benefits are subject to certain limitations. For more information on all covered services and detailed information on benefit levels, limitations, exclusions, program policies, and payments for nonnetwork and overseas dentists, please see the Enhanced Program Benefits Booklet and Enhanced-Overseas TRDP supplement.

Dentist network

As an enrolled member of the Enhanced TRDP, you can save the most on your out-of-pocket expenses by choosing a participating TRDP dentist network in one of more than 150,000 locations nationwide. If you go to a non-TRDP network dentist, Delta Dental pays the same percentage of covered services but cannot guarantee the dentist's fees. Nonnetwork dentists will bill you for their normal fees, which may be higher than the program's allowed amount for the service. You will be responsible for paying your copayment plus any difference between the program's allowed amount and the dentist's billed charge.

Delta Dental does not maintain a participating TRDP dentist network overseas. Enhanced-Overseas TRDP enrollees who need to locate a dentist

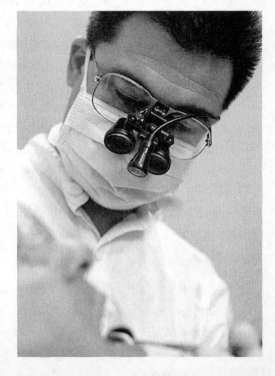

for covered services or are traveling overseas and need emergency dental treatment and dependents of Enhanced TRDP enrollees who are full-time students studying overseas can search a list of dentists and dental clinics in virtually every country, provided through Delta Dental's international dentist referral service. Enrollees also may select an overseas dentist from the overseas host nation provider search tool located on the program's website (**www.trdp. org**). Dentists listed with Delta Dental's international dentist referral service and on the overseas host nation provider search tool are not contracted or otherwise affiliated with Delta Dental.

Enrollment

Enrollment in the TRDP is voluntary. Each new enrollee must fulfill an initial enrollment period of 12 consecutive months. After the initial 12-month period, you become eligible for the full scope of benefits offered under the Enhanced TRDP and will continue your enrollment in the program on a month-to-month basis.

There is a grace period of 30 days from your coverage effective date during which you may rescind your enrollment agreement without any further obligation, provided you have not used any program services during that time. If you do not exercise your option to rescind within the 30-day grace period, you must remain enrolled in the program for the duration of the initial 12-month period without further opportunity for voluntary disenrollment.

If you are a new retiree who elects to enroll within four months after your retirement from active duty or transfer to Retired Reserve status, you are eligible for a waiver of the 12-month waiting period for the full scope of benefits. Eligibility for this waiver includes retirees of the National Guard/Reserve in the "gray area" who are entitled to retired pay but will not begin receiving it until age 60. A copy of your retirement orders, confirmation of your transfer to Retired Reserve status, or Chronological History of Drill Points must be submitted with your enrollment application to verify your eligibility for this waiver. Additionally, if you are retiring soon from the Uniformed Services and wish to enroll in the TRDP with no gap in coverage, it is recommended that you do so in the month before your retirement date to ensure your coverage under the TRDP begins as soon as your retirement is effective.

A two-month premium prepayment in U.S. dollars is required at the time of enrollment to ensure you and all enrolled family members can receive benefits the first day your coverage becomes effective. Once your mandatory allotment is established, any unused portion of the prepayment will be refunded to you during the first few months of your enrollment.

There are three ways to enroll in the TRDP: online, by telephone, or by mail. To avoid delays in delivering and processing mail, online or telephone enrollment is strongly recommended, especially for enrollees in the Enhanced-Overseas TRDP. Coverage will begin on the first day of the month following the acceptance of your enrollment application and a two-month premium prepayment.

Once your enrollment is processed, you will receive a welcome packet containing your program identification cards, Enhanced Program Benefits Booklet, and other pertinent information by mail. Or, you have the option of receiving access to your welcome packet materials electronically by providing your email address when you enroll.

Your coverage begins the first day of the month following your enrollment, regardless of whether you have received your welcome packet.

Cost

The TRDP has been designed to provide you and your family with comprehensive dental benefits at an affordable cost. Monthly premium amounts for enrollees in the Enhanced TRDP will vary depending on where you live and the number of family members you elect to enroll. Although monthly premium amounts for enrollees in the Enhanced-Overseas TRDP do not vary by region, they are based the enrollment option selected.

Premium rates will change slightly on October 1 of each benefit year. To find out your current premium rate, use this website to search by your location: **http://trdp.org/pro/premiumSrch.html**.

Federal law mandates that monthly premiums for the TRDP be deducted automatically from Uniformed Services retired pay.

TRICARE Pharmacy Program

TRICARE prescription drug coverage is available to all TRICARE-eligible beneficiaries who are enrolled in DEERS. Prescription drug coverage is the same regardless of which health plan option you are using, and it is available worldwide. TRICARE provides pharmacy benefits to all eligible uniformed service members, retirees, and family members, including beneficiaries age 65 and older.

Your coverage is the same regardless of your beneficiary category or which health plan option you are using. The TRICARE Pharmacy Program is available worldwide, however there are some limitations to having your prescriptions filled in some overseas areas.

Eligible beneficiaries include:

- Active duty service members and their families
- Activated National Guard and Reserve Members and their families (on Title 10 or Title 32 [federal] orders)
- Retired service members and their families
- Retired National Guard and Reserve members and their families (age 60 and above and receiving retired pay)
- Survivors, widows/widowers, and certain former spouses
- Medal of Honor recipients and their families
- Beneficiaries enrolled in TRICARE Reserve Select or the Continued Health Care Benefit Program
- Other beneficiaries listed in DEERS as eligible for TRICARE, including foreign force members and their families

Filling prescriptions

TRICARE offers several convenient ways for you to have prescriptions filled depending on your family's specific needs. You can have prescriptions filled at any of these pharmacies based on your specific situation, and you can use more than one option at a time.

- Military pharmacy: least expensive option with no out-of-pocket costs
- Mail order pharmacy: safe, convenient, and the most cost-effective option when a military pharmacy is not available
- Network pharmacy: more than 54,000 network pharmacies in the United States and U.S. territories
- Nonnetwork pharmacy: most expensive option

Although each option is available worldwide, some may be limited outside of the United States.

TRICARE covers most U.S. Food and Drug Administration (FDA)-approved prescription medications. Medications may be available as part of the pharmacy or medical benefit. In general, for a medication to be covered by the TRICARE pharmacy benefit, it must:

- Be a prescription medication approved by the FDA
- Not be part of a procedure covered under the medical benefit
- Be prescribed in accordance with good medical practice and established standards of quality

Additionally, medications that are not medically or psychologically necessary for the diagnosis or treatment of a covered illness are not covered by TRICARE. Prescription medications used to treat conditions that are not currently covered by TRICARE either by statute or regulation likewise are excluded from the pharmacy benefit. Excluded medications include:

- Drugs prescribed for cosmetic purposes
- Fluoride preparations
- Food supplements
- Homeopathic and herbal preparations
- Multivitamins
- Over-the-counter (OTC) products, except for the following:
  o Insulin and diabetic supplies
  o OTC medications covered by the OTC Medication Demonstration Project

- Smoking cessation products
- Weight reduction products

Over-the-counter prenatal vitamins are not covered; however, if you have a prescription for prenatal vitamins, they are covered by TRICARE.

Pharmacy costs are based on whether the prescription is classified as a formulary generic (Tier 1), formulary brand name (Tier 2), or non-formulary (Tier 3) drug, and where you choose to have your prescription filled.

Benefits Under the TRICARE Programs

TRICARE offers comprehensive, affordable health coverage with several health plan options, a robust pharmacy benefit, dental options, and other special programs. This section will cover many of the procedures TRICARE will help you pay.

Eye exams

TRICARE covers one comprehensive ophthalmologic eye exam every two years when enrolled in TRICARE Prime. You can receive these eye exams from a TRICARE-authorized optometrist or ophthalmologist.

If you see a TRICARE network provider, you do not need a referral from your primary care manager. If you see a TRICARE nonnetwork provider, you must have a referral from your primary care manager or the care will be denied.

Well-child benefit

Through the well-child benefit, children (regardless of plan) are covered for one eye and vision screening (testing for visual acuity, ocular alignment, and red reflex) at birth and at 6 months old by their primary/pediatric provider and two comprehensive eye exams (including screening for amblyopia and strabismus) between the ages of 3 and 6. After age 6, they receive one comprehensive eye exam every two years.

Mental health and behavior

TRICARE covers mental health/behavioral health care that is medically or psychologically necessary for treatment of a behavioral health disorder.

Outpatient services

Referrals and authorizations may apply for certain outpatient services (does not apply to ADSMs receiving care at an MTF). Care access and rules vary by beneficiary type, location, and TRICARE program option.

Psychotherapy

Psychotherapy is an interpersonal, discussion-based type of behavioral health care. When medically or psychologically necessary to treat a behavioral health disorder, outpatient and inpatient psychotherapy is covered. Outpatient psychotherapy is covered up to two sessions per week in any combination of individual, family, collateral, or group sessions. Inpatient psychotherapy is covered up to five sessions per week in any combination of sessions. The duration and frequency of additional care is dependent upon medical necessity. The following therapy sessions are covered:

- Individual psychotherapy: Therapy may be used for adults and children to ease emotional issues, reverse or change troubling behavior, and encourage personality growth and development. Sessions are covered up to 60 minutes; crisis sessions may extend up to 120 minutes. Individual psychotherapy is not a covered benefit for a patient with a diagnosis of substance abuse unless the person also has a mental disorder diagnosis.

- Play therapy: A form of covered individual psychotherapy used to diagnose and treat children

- Family or conjoint psychotherapy: Therapy is designed to treat the entire family. Regular sessions are covered for up to 90 minutes; crisis sessions may extend up to 180 minutes.

- Group psychotherapy: Sessions are covered for up to 90 minutes.

- Collateral visits: A collateral visit is not a therapy session. These visits are used to gather information and to implement treatment goals. Collateral visits are counted as individual psychotherapy sessions and can last up to 60 minutes. Beneficiaries have the option of combining a collateral visit with another individual or group psychotherapy visit.

Psychoanalysis

Psychoanalysis differs from psychotherapy and requires prior authorization. After prior authorization is obtained, it is covered when administered by a graduate or candidate of a psychoanalytic training institution.

Psychological testing

Psychological testing and assessment is covered only when provided in conjunction with psychotherapy. Testing is limited to six hours per fiscal year (October 1–September 30). Any testing more than six hours requires a review for medical necessity.

Inpatient services

Availability, care access, referral, and authorization requirements for inpatient services may vary by beneficiary type, location, and TRICARE program option. Refer to the Getting Care section for those details. Prior authorization is required for all nonemergency inpatient behavioral health care services. In emergencies, authorization is required for continued stay.

Acute inpatient psychiatric care

Patients may be referred to acute inpatient psychiatric care if their doctor believes they have a behavioral health disorder that threatens their physical well-being to the extent that 24-hour medical and psychiatric care is needed.

Benefit Limits:

- Patients 19 and older are limited to 30 days per fiscal year or in any single admission.

- Patients 18 and younger are limited to 45 days per fiscal year or in any single admission.

Psychiatric partial hospitalization program

A psychiatric partial hospitalization program (PHP) is recommended when your physician believes it is necessary to stabilize a critical behavioral health disorder or to transition from an inpatient program to an outpatient program. A PHP is a treatment setting providing medical therapeutic services at least three hours per day, five days per week. Treatment may include day, evening, night, and weekend programs.

TRICARE provides up to 60 days of coverage per FY (full- or half-day program) in a TRICARE-authorized program for behavioral health disorders. PHP treatment for a diagnosis of a substance use disorder is limited to the rehabilitation treatment maximum outlined in "Substance Use Disorders." PHP care does not count toward the 30- or 45-day limit for acute inpatient psychiatric care.

Substance use disorders

Substance use disorders include alcohol or drug abuse or dependence. Services are covered only by TRICARE-authorized institutional providers — an authorized hospital or an organized treatment program in an authorized freestanding or hospital-based substance use disorder rehabilitation facility (SUDRF). Treatment includes detoxification, rehabilitation, and outpatient individual, group, and family therapy.

TRICARE covers three substance use disorder rehabilitation treatments in a lifetime and one per benefit period. A benefit period begins with the first date of the covered treatment and ends 365 days later.

Detoxification (emergency inpatient)

TRICARE covers emergency inpatient chemical detoxification treatment when the patient's condition requires the personnel and facilities of a hospital or SUDRF. Up to seven days per episode is covered in a TRICARE-authorized facility. TRICARE may cover more days if determined to be medically or psychologically necessary. Inpatient detoxification care counts toward the 30- or 45-day limit for acute inpatient psychiatric care but not toward the rehabilitation level of care.

Rehabilitation

Rehabilitation of a substance use disorder may occur in an inpatient or partial hospitalization setting. TRICARE covers 21 days of rehabilitation per benefit period in a TRICARE-authorized facility, whether an inpatient or partial hospitalization or a combination of both. Inpatient days for rehabilitation count toward the 30- or 45-day limit for acute inpatient psychiatric care and partial hospitalization days count toward the 60-day limit for partial hospitalization.

Outpatient care

Outpatient care must be provided in an individual or group setting by an approved SUDRF (free-standing or hospital-based). Benefit limits are as follows:

- Individual and group therapy: up to 60 visits per benefit period
- Family therapy: up to 15 visits per benefit period. Limits may be waived if more visits are deemed medically or psychologically necessary.

TRICARE Young Adult (TYA)

TRICARE Young Adult is a premium-based health care plan that qualified dependents may purchase. TRICARE Young Adult provides medical and pharmacy benefits, but dental coverage is excluded.

TRICARE Young Adult allows dependent adult children to purchase TRICARE coverage after eligibility for "regular" TRICARE coverage ends at age 21 (or 23 if enrolled in a full course of study at an approved institution of higher learning). The option you select when you enroll (Prime or Standard) determines how you get care.

You may qualify to purchase TRICARE Young Adult if you are:

- An adult child of an eligible sponsor
- Eligible sponsors include:
  - o   Active duty service members
  - o   Retired service members
  - o   Activated Guard/Reserve members
  - o   Non-activated Guard/Reserve members using TRICARE Reserve Select
  - o   Retired Guard/Reserve members using TRICARE Retired Reserve
- Unmarried
- At least age 21 but not yet 26 years old

Note: If you are enrolled in a full course of study at an approved institution of higher learning and your sponsor provides 50 percent of your financial support, your eligibility may not begin until age 23 or upon graduation, whichever comes first.

- Not eligible to enroll in an employer-sponsored health plan based on your own employment
- Not otherwise eligible for TRICARE program coverage

Monthly premiums and out-of-pocket costs

To participate, you must pay monthly premiums. TRICARE Young Adult premium rates are established annually on a calendar year basis. The current monthly premium amounts are as follows for each option:

- Prime Option: $201 per month
- Standard Option: $176 per month

Your out-of-pocket health care costs are then determined by the option you select when you enroll, Prime or Standard. When using the Standard option your costs will also vary based on your sponsor's military status and the type of provider you see. For more information, visit the TRICARE Young Adult website at **www.tricare.mil/mybenefit/home/overview/ LearnAboutPlansAndCosts/TRICAREYoungAdult?p=TYA**.

Special Programs

TRICARE offers supplemental programs tailored specifically to beneficiary health concerns or conditions. Many of these programs have specific eligibility requirements based on beneficiary category, plan, or status.

These programs include health promotion programs such as alcohol education, smoking cessation and weight loss. Some are for specific beneficiary populations such as the Foreign Force Member Health Care Option and the Pre-activation Benefit for National Guard and Reserve. Other programs are for specific health conditions such as the Cancer Clinical Trials. Many programs are limited to a certain number of participants or a certain geographic location such as chiropractic care. Details on these programs are available at **www.tricare.mil**.

Chapter 6

CHAMPVA Health Care Program

The Civilian Health and Medical Program of the Department of Veterans Affairs (CHAMPVA) is a comprehensive health care program in which the VA shares the cost of covered health care services and supplies with eligible beneficiaries. The program is administered by Health Administration Center with offices in Denver, Colorado.

Due to the similarity between CHAMPVA and the TRICARE program, the two are often mistaken for each other. CHAMPVA is a Department of Veterans Affairs program whereas TRICARE is a regionally managed health care program for active duty and retired members of the uniformed services, their families, and survivors. In some cases, a veterans may look to be eligible for both/either program on paper. However, if you are a military retiree, or the spouse of a veteran who was killed in action, you are and will always be a TRICARE beneficiary, you cannot choose between the two.

CHAMPVA Overview

The CHAMPVA program covers most health care services and supplies that are medically and psychologically necessary. Upon confirmation of eligibility, you will receive a CHAMPVA handbook that specifically addresses covered and non-covered services and supplies.

As with all health programs, certain services and supplies are not covered. Some of these are:

- Services and supplies obtained as part of a grant, study, or research program
- Services and supplies not provided in accordance with accepted professional medical standards or related to experimental/investigational or unproven procedures or treatment regimens
- Care for which you are not obligated to pay, such as services obtained at a health fair
- Care provided outside the scope of the provider's license or certification
- Services or supplies above the appropriate level required to provide the necessary medical care
- Services by providers suspended or sanctioned by any federal agency
- Services provided by a member of your immediate family or person living in your household

For a complete listing of non-covered services and supplies, consult the CHAMVPA handbook, which is available on the VA website (**www.va.gov**).

Program eligibility

To be eligible for CHAMPVA, you cannot be eligible for TRICARE, and you must be in one of these categories:

- The spouse or child of a veteran who has been rated permanently and totally disabled for a service-connected disability by a VA regional office

- The surviving spouse or child of a veteran who died from a VA-rated service connected disability

- The surviving spouse or child of a veteran who was at the time of death rated permanently and totally disabled from a service connected disability

- The surviving spouse or child of a military member who died in the line of duty, not due to misconduct (in most of these cases, these family members are eligible for TRICARE, not CHAMPVA)

NOTE: The eligibility of a child is not affected by the divorce or remarriage of the spouse except in the case of a stepchild. When a stepchild leaves the sponsor's household, the child is no longer eligible for CHAMPVA.

Medicare Impact

CHAMPVA is always the secondary payer to Medicare. If you are eligible for CHAMPVA, under age 65, and enrolled in both Medicare Parts A&B, SSA documentation of enrollment in both Parts A&B is required. *Medicare was discussed in Chapter 5.*

For your benefits to be extended past age 65, you must meet the following conditions:

- If the beneficiary was 65 or older before June 5, 2001, was otherwise eligible for CHAMPVA, and was entitled to Medicare Part A coverage, then the beneficiary will be eligible for CHAMPVA without having to have Medicare Part B coverage.
- If you turned 65 on or before June 5, 2001, and have Medicare Parts A and B, you must keep both Parts to be eligible.

- If you turned 65 on or after June 5, 2001, you must be enrolled in Medicare Parts A and B to be eligible.
- You are not required to enroll in Medicare Part D in order to become or remain CHAMPVA eligible.

An eligible CHAMPVA sponsor may be entitled to receive medical care through the VA health care system based on his or her own veteran status. Additionally, if the eligible CHAMPVA sponsor is the spouse of another eligible CHAMPVA sponsor, both may now be eligible for CHAMPVA benefits. In each instance where the eligible spouse requires medical attention, he or she may choose the VA health care system or coverage under CHAMPVA for his or her health care needs.

Remarriage

Eligibility for CHAMPVA ends at midnight on the date of your remarriage if you remarry before age 55. If you remarry on or after your 55th birthday, you can keep your CHAMPVA benefits.

If you are a widow(er) of a qualifying sponsor, you remarry, and the remarriage is later terminated by death, divorce, or annulment, you may reestablish CHAMPVA eligibility. The beginning date of your re-eligibility is the first day of the month after termination of the remarriage. To reestablish CHAMPVA eligibility, copies of the marriage certificate and death, divorce, or annulment documents must be provided.

New and expectant parents

If you are expecting and you need to establish CHAMPVA eligibility for your new child, the following must be accomplished before you can submit an application.

- Obtain a Social Security number for the newborn by applying to the nearest Social Security Administration office.

- Establish dependency of the newborn to the veteran sponsor by contacting the local VA regional office.

Because the payment of claims for this child is contingent upon his or her eligibility status, as new parents, you are encouraged to take the above action as early as possible.

CHAMPVA Assistance and Claims Address

The VA does not maintain a provider listing. Most Medicare and TRI-CARE providers also will accept CHAMPVA (but be sure you ask the provider). If you are having difficulty finding a provider, we recommend you visit the Medicare website **www.medicare.gov** and use the "Search Tools" at the bottom of that page to locate a Medicare provider. You also may visit the TRICARE website at **www.tricare.mil/standardprovider** to locate a provider in your area. If you choose to see a provider who does not accept CHAMPVA, you likely will have to pay the entire bill and then submit a claim for reimbursement of our cost share. Remember that CHAMPVA cost shares are based on the CHAMPVA allowable amount.

CHAMPVA Inhouse Treatment Initiative (CITI)

The CHAMPVA Inhouse Treatment Initiative is a voluntary program that allows for you, the CHAMPVA beneficiary, to be treated at participating VA medical centers with no out-of-pocket cost. Each VA medical center that participates in the CITI program offers different services based on unused capacity. Once you locate a CITI facility that you want to use, contact the CITI coordinator to find out what services are offered at that specific medical center. Unfortunately however, if you are a CHAMPVA beneficiary who is also covered by Medicare, you cannot participate in the CITI program because Medicare does not pay for services provided by a VA Medical Center. A brochure is available at **www.va.gov/hac/forbeneficiaries/champva/brochure/CITI-Brochure.pdf**.

CHAMPVA Pharmacy Benefits

The CHAMPVA program offers a robust pharmacy benefit and pays 75 percent of the allowable charge at any pharmacy for prescription medication. CHAMPVA also offers a medication by mail program called MEDS BY MAIL.

Pharmacies that accept CHAMPVA

Pharmacies that accept the CHAMPVA card agree to collect your cost share and send a claim to CHAMPVA for the remaining amount. However, not all pharmacies accept the CHAMPVA card. In those cases, you may have to pay the entire amount and submit a claim to CHAMPVA yourself. A good way to find a pharmacy that accepts the CHAMPVA card is to use the MEDICAL MATRIX network.

Meds by Mail

The Meds By Mail program offers prescription medication delivered to your home. The best part of Meds By Mail is that there is *no* cost share or copay. Detailed information is available at **www.va.gov/hac/forbeneficia-ries/meds/meds.asp**.

Other Health Insurance (OHI) and CHAMPVA

If you have other health insurance, you must notify the Health Administration Center of any changes (dropped insurance, changes in health plans, etc) immediately upon those changes taking effect so proper payment to your claims can be made. If you obtain a major medical policy, you also must notify the Health Administration Center that you have a new policy and when it takes effect.

The CHAMPVA Handbook contains important benefit information. You are highly encouraged to carefully read the handbook before using CHAMPVA benefits. You can download it from **www.va.gov/hac/forben-eficiaries/champva/handbook/chandbook.pdf**.

You can read more about CHAMPVA by visiting the fact sheets and CHAMPVA Handbook posted on the VA website: **www.va.gov**.

Chapter 7

Disability Benefits and Compensation

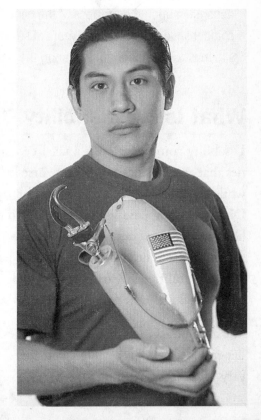

The war in Iraq and Afghanistan has placed a spotlight on the treatment of our honored service members who have paid a severe price for their sacrifice and service. But even before the increased media attention on how our disabled veterans are cared for, the VA implemented many programs and set up special compensation for those who have been injured during their active duty defending our country.

Chapter 2 outlined the process for determining disability and how the disability percentages are computed. This chapter will give more information and details about how you can use your status to receive more benefits and entitlements you are entitled to receive because of your distinguished record.

Differences Between Military Disability Ratings and VA Disability Ratings

Although the Department of Defense and the VA use the VA Schedule for Rating Disabilities, not all the general policy provisions set forth in the Rating Schedule apply to the military. Consequently, disability ratings may vary between the two. The military rates only conditions determined to be physically unfitting and thus compensates for the loss of a military career. The VA may rate any service-connected impairment and compensate for loss of civilian employability. Another difference is the term of the rating. The military's ratings are permanent upon final disposition. VA ratings may fluctuate with time, depending upon the progress of the condition. Further, the military's disability compensation is affected by years of service and basic pay, while VA compensation is a flat amount based upon the percentage rating received.

What Is VA Disability Compensation?

Disability compensation is a tax-free benefit paid to a veteran for disabilities that are a result of or made worse by injuries or diseases that happened while on active duty, active duty for training, or inactive duty training. Disability compensation also is paid to certain veterans disabled from VA health care. This compensation varies with the degree of disability and the number of veteran's dependents and is paid monthly. Veterans with certain severe disabilities may be eligible for additional special monthly compensation. The benefits are not subject to federal or state income tax.

The amount of basic benefit paid ranges from $123 to $2,673 per month, depending on how disabled you are. The following chart illustrates the varying rates for veterans.

2011 VA Disability Compensation Rates for Veterans	
Veteran's Disability Rating	**Monthly Rate Paid to Veterans**
10 percent	$123
20 percent	$243
30 percent*	$376
40 percent*	$541
50 percent*	$770
60 percent*	$974
70 percent*	$1,228
80 percent*	$1,427
90 percent*	$1,604
100 percent*	$2,673

*Veterans with disability ratings of at least 30 percent are eligible for additional allowances for dependents, including spouses, minor children, children between the ages of 18 and 23 who are attending school, children who are permanently incapable of self-support because of a disability arising before age 18, and dependent parents. The additional amount depends on the disability rating and the number of dependents.

The payment of military retirement pay, disability severance pay, and separation incentive payments known as SSB (Special Separation Benefits) and VSI (Voluntary Separation Incentives) affects the amount of VA compensation paid to disabled veterans. The VA offers three payment options to veterans eligible to receive benefit payments. Most veterans receive their payments by direct deposit to a bank, savings and loan, or credit union account. In some areas, veterans who do not have a bank account can open a federally insured Electronic Transfer Account, which costs about $3 a month, provides a monthly statement, and allows cash withdrawals. Other veterans may choose to receive benefits by check.

You may be paid additional amounts, in certain instances, if:

- You have very severe disabilities or loss of limb(s)
- You have a spouse, child(ren), or dependent parent(s)
- You have a seriously disabled spouse

You can apply by filling out VA Form 21-526, Veterans Application for Compensation and/or Pension available at **www.vba.va.gov/pubs/forms/vba-21-526-are.pdf** or online through the VA website at **www.vba.va.gov/bln/21**.

"Presumptive" disability benefits

Even if you do not have proof that your active duty caused your disability, if it was a side effect of your time in the military, you still might be eligible for compensation. The VA *presumes* that specific disabilities diagnosed in certain veterans were caused by their military service. If one of these conditions is diagnosed in a veteran in one of the following groups, VA will assume the circumstances of his or her service caused the condition, and disability compensation can be awarded.

Veterans diagnosed with chronic diseases (such as arthritis, diabetes, or hypertension) are encouraged to apply for disability compensation. Being diagnosed with amyotrophic lateral sclerosis (ALS)/Lou Gehrig's disease at any time after discharge or release from qualifying active service is sufficient to establish service connection for the disease, if the veteran had active, continuous service of 90 days or more.

The following chart enumerates many of the illnesses or disabilities and their possible causes that the VA will allow under these presumptive benefits.

Former Prisoners of War	Vietnam Veterans (Exposed to Agent Orange)	Atomic Veterans (Exposed to Ionizing Radiation)	Gulf War Veterans (Undiagnosed Illness)
(1) *Imprisoned for any length of time with a disability at least 10 percent disabling:* • Psychosis • Any of the anxiety states • Dysthymic disorder • Organic residuals of frostbite • Post-traumatic osteoarthritis	Served in the Republic of Vietnam between Jan. 9, 1962, and May 7, 1975: • Acute and subacute peripheral neuropathy* • AL amyloidosis • B-cell leukemias • Chloracne or other acneform disease similar to chloracne*	Participated in atmospheric nuclear testing; occupied or was a POW in Hiroshima or Nagasaki; service before Feb. 1, 1992, at a diffusion plant in Paducah, KY, Portsmouth, OH, or Oak Ridge, TN; or service before Jan. 1, 1974, at Amchitka Island, AK: • All forms of leukemia (except	Served in the Southwest Asia Theater of Operations during the Gulf War with condition at least 10 percent disabling by December 31, 2011. Included are medically unexplained chronic multi-symptom illnesses defined by a cluster of signs or symptoms that have existed for six months or more, such as:

Former Prisoners of War	Vietnam Veterans (Exposed to Agent Orange)	Atomic Veterans (Exposed to Ionizing Radiation)	Gulf War Veterans (Undiagnosed Illness)
• Heart disease or hypertensive vascular disease and their complications • Stroke and its residuals **(2)** *Imprisoned for at least 30 days, and disability at least 10 percent disabling:* • Avitaminosis • Beriberi • Chronic dysentery • Helminthiasis • Malnutrition (including optic atrophy) • Pellagra • Any other nutritional deficiency • Irritable bowel syndrome • Peptic ulcer disease • Peripheral neuropathy • Cirrhosis of the liver	• Chronic lymphocytic leukemia • Diabetes type 2 • Hodgkin's disease • Ischemic heart disease • Multiple myeloma • Non-Hodgkin's lymphoma • Parkinson's disease • Porphyria cutanea tarda* • Prostate cancer • Respiratory cancers (lung, bronchus, larynx, trachea) • Soft-tissue sarcoma (other than osteosarcoma, chondrosar-coma, Kaposi's sarcoma or mesothelioma) *Must become manifest to a degree of 10 percent or more within a year after the last date on which the veteran was exposed to an herbicide agent during active military, naval, or air service.	for chronic lymphocytic leukemia) • Cancer of the thyroid, breast, pharynx, esoph-agus, stomach, small intestine, pancreas, bile ducts, gall bladder, salivary gland, urinary tract (kidneys, renal pelves, ureters, urinary bladder and urethra), brain, bone, lung, colon, ovary • Bronchiolo-alveolar carcinoma • Multiple myeloma • Lymphomas (other than Hodgkin's disease) • Primary liver cancer (except if cirrhosis or hepatitis B is indicated)	• Chronic fatigue syndrome • Fibromyalgia • Irritable bowel syndrome • Any diagnosed or undiagnosed illness that the secretary of veterans affairs determines warrants a presumption of service connection *Signs or symptoms of an undiagnosed illness include:* fatigue, skin symptoms, head-aches, muscle pain, joint pain, neurologi-cal symptoms, respi-ratory symptoms, sleep disturbance, GI symptoms, cardio-vascular symptoms, weight loss, men-strual disorders

Compensation Programs

Depending on the severity of your disability, your status in the military, if your disability stems from combat, and your income, you might be eligible for additional compensation programs from the VA. This section will cover these additional programs and help you decide if you could qualify for additional aid.

Concurrent Retirement and Disability Payments (CRDP)

Concurrent Retirement and Disability Payments (CRDP) restore retired pay on a graduated ten-year schedule for retirees with a 50 to 90 percent VA-rated disability. Concurrent retirement payments increase 10 percent per year through 2013. Veterans rated 100-percent disabled by VA are entitled to full CRDP without being phased in.

To qualify, veterans also must meet all three of the following criteria:

- Have 20 or more years on active duty, or a reservist age 60 or older with 20 or more creditable years
- Be in a retired status
- Be receiving retired pay (must be offset by VA payments)

Concurrent Retirement and Disability Pay (CRDP) allows military retirees to receive both military retired pay and Veterans Affairs (VA) compensation. CRDP is a "phase in" of benefits that gradually restores a retiree's VA disability offset. This means that an eligible retiree's retired pay will increase gradually each year until the phase in is complete in 2014.

You do not need to apply for CRDP. If qualified, you will be enrolled automatically. You must be eligible for retired pay to qualify for CRDP. If you were placed on a disability retirement but would be eligible for military retired pay in the absence of the disability, you may be entitled to receive CRDP.

Under these rules, you may be entitled to CRDP if:

- You are a regular retiree with a VA disability rating of 50 percent or greater.

- You are a reserve retiree with 20 qualifying years of service, who has a VA disability rating of 50 percent or greater and who has reached retirement age. (In most cases, the retirement age for reservists is 60, but certain reserve retirees may be eligible before they turn 60. If you are a member of the Ready Reserve, your retirement age can be reduced below age 60 by three months for each 90 days of active service you have performed during a fiscal year.)

- You are retired under Temporary Early Retirement Act (TERA) and have a VA disability rating of 50 percent or greater.

- You are a disability retiree who earned entitlement to retired pay under any provision of law other than solely by disability, and you have a VA disability rating of 50 percent or greater. You might become eligible for CRDP at the time you would have become eligible for retired pay.

In addition to monthly CRDP payments, you may be eligible for a retroactive payment. Your retroactive payment date may go as far back as January 1, 2004, but can be limited based on:

- Your retirement date or
- When you first increased to at least 50 percent disability rating
- No CRDP is payable for any month before January 2004.

You are eligible for full concurrent receipt of both your VA disability compensation and your retired pay, if you are a military retiree who meets all of the above eligibility requirements in addition to both of the following:

- You are rated by the VA as unemployable, generally referred to as Individual Unemployability (IU).
- You are in receipt of VA disability compensation because of IU.
- This is retroactive to January 1, 2005.

Combat-Related Special Compensation (CRSC) for retired veterans

Combat-Related Special Compensation (CRSC) provides tax-free monthly payments to eligible retired veterans with combat-related injuries. With CRSC, veterans can receive both their full military retirement pay and their VA disability compensation if the injury is combat-related.

Retired veterans with combat-related injuries must meet all of the following criteria to apply for CRSC:

- Active, reserve, or medically retired with 20 years of creditable service
- Receive military retired pay
- Have a 10 percent or greater VA-rated injury
- Military retired pay is reduced by VA disability payments (VA waiver)

In addition, veterans must be able to provide documentary evidence that their injuries were a result of one of the following:

- Training that simulates war (e.g., exercises, field training)
- Hazardous duty (e.g., flight, diving, parachute duty)
- An instrumentality of war (e.g. combat vehicles, weapons, Agent Orange)
- Armed conflict (e.g. gunshot wounds {Purple Heart}, punji stick injuries)

For more information, visit the website **www.military.com/benefits/content/military-pay/special-pay/combat-related-special-compensation.html**. Use the following form to apply: **www.eglin.af.mil/shared/media/document/AFD-080905-039.pdf**.

Improved disability pension for low income veterans

Veterans with low incomes who are permanently and totally disabled, or who are age 65 and older, may be eligible for monetary support if they have at least 90 days of active military service, at least one day of which was during a period of war. Veterans who entered active duty on or after Sept. 8, 1980, or officers who entered active duty on or after Oct. 16, 1981, may have to meet a longer minimum period of active duty. The veteran's discharge must have been under conditions other than dishonorable, and the disability must be for reasons other than the veteran's own willful misconduct.

Congress establishes the maximum annual improved disability pension rates. Payments are reduced by the amount of countable income of the veteran, spouse, and dependent children. When a veteran without a spouse or a child is furnished nursing home or domiciliary care by VA, the pension is reduced to an amount not to exceed $90 per month after three calendar months of care. The reduction may be delayed if nursing-home care is being continued to provide the veteran with rehabilitation services.

2013 VA Improved Disability Pension Rates	
Status of Veteran's Family Situation and Caretaking Needs	Maximum Annual Rate
Veteran without dependents	$12,444
Veteran with one dependent	$16,308

2013 VA Improved Disability Pension Rates	
Veteran permanently housebound, no dependents	$15,108
Veteran permanently housebound, one dependent	$18,840
Veteran needing regular aid and attendance, no dependents	$13,344
Veteran needing regular aid and attendance, one dependent	$15,024
Two veterans married to one another	$16,308
Increase for each additional dependent child	$2,112

Payments are made to bring the veteran's total income, including other retirement or Social Security income, to a level set by Congress. Un-reimbursed medical expenses may reduce countable income for VA purposes. Additional information can be found in the Compensation and Pension Benefits section of VA's Internet pages at **www.vba.va.gov/bln/21**.

Protected pension

Pension beneficiaries who were receiving a VA pension on Dec. 31, 1978, and do not wish to elect the Improved Pension will continue to receive the pension rate they were receiving on that date. This rate generally continues as long as the beneficiary's income remains within established limits, his or her net worth does not bar payment, and the beneficiary does not lose any dependents.

These beneficiaries must continue to meet basic eligibility factors, such as permanent and total disability for veterans or status as a surviving spouse or child. VA must adjust rates for other reasons, such as a veteran's hospitalization in a VA facility.

Special Monthly Compensation (SMC) for serious disabilities

The VA will pay additional compensation to a veteran who, because of military service, incurred the loss or loss of use of specific organs or extremities. Loss, or loss of use, is described as either an amputation or, having no effective remaining function of an extremity or organ. The disabilities VA will consider for SMC include:

- Loss, or loss of use, of a hand or foot
- Immobility of a joint or paralysis
- Loss of sight of an eye (having only light perception)
- Loss, or loss of use, of a reproductive organ
- Complete loss, or loss of use, of both buttocks
- Deafness of both ears (having absence of air and bone conduction)
- Inability to communicate by speech (complete organic aphonia)
- Loss of a percentage of tissue from a single breast, or both breasts, from mastectomy or radiation treatment

The VA will pay higher rates for combinations of these disabilities such as loss or loss of use of the feet, legs, hands, and arms, in specific monetary increments, based on the particular combination of the disabilities. There are also higher payments for various combinations of severe deafness with bilateral blindness. Additional SMC is available if a veteran has service-connected paraplegia, with complete loss of bowel and bladder control.

In addition, if you have other service-connected disabilities that, in combination with the above special monthly compensation, meet certain criteria, a higher amount of SMC also can be considered.

If a veteran is service connected at the 100 percent rate and is housebound, is bedridden, or is so helpless as to need the aid and attendance of another person, then consideration of payment of additional SMC can be considered. The amount of SMC will vary depending on the level of aid and attendance needed.

Contact your local VA regional office for information about applying for SMC or apply online at **www.va.gov**.

Compensation for sexual or personal trauma

A number of women and men suffered sexual or other personal trauma while serving in the military. These veterans still may struggle with fear, anxiety, embarrassment, or profound anger because of these experiences. Sexual or personal trauma are events of human design that threaten or inflict harm. Trauma is defined as any lingering physical, emotional, or psychological symptoms. Examples of trauma are:

- Rape
- Physical assault
- Domestic battering
- Stalking

If it is determined that your disabilities are a result of or have been made worse by injuries or diseases incurred during military service, you may receive compensation. You must have been separated under other than dishonorable conditions to be eligible and must currently suffer from a disabling condition. You can apply for disability compensation by filling out VA Form 21-526, Veterans Application for Compensation and/or Pension available at **www.vba.va.gov/pubs/forms/vba-21-526-are.pdf**. VA counselors and women veterans coordinators are available for assistance. You also can apply online at **http://vabenefits.vba.va.gov/vonapp**.

Housebound compensation

A veteran who is determined by VA to be in need of the regular aid and attendance of another person or a veteran who is permanently housebound may be entitled to additional disability compensation or pension payments. A veteran evaluated at 30 percent or more disabled is entitled to receive an additional payment for a spouse who is in need of the aid and attendance of another person.

Individual unemployability compensation

Individual unemployability is a part of VA's disability compensation program that allows the VA to pay certain veterans compensation at the 100 percent rate, even though VA has not rated their service-connected disabilities at the total level.

A veteran must be unable to maintain substantially gainful employment because of his other service-connected disabilities. Additionally, a veteran must have one service-connected disability ratable at 60 percent or more, or two or more service-connected disabilities, at least one disability ratable at 40 percent or more with a combined rating of 70 percent or more.

To apply, submit VA Form 21-8940, Veteran's Application for Increased Compensation Based on Unemployability, to your nearest VA Regional Office.

Veterans who are in receipt of individual unemployability benefits may work as long as it is not considered substantially gainful employment. The employment must be considered marginal employment. Substantially gainful employment is defined as employment at which nondisabled individuals earn their livelihood with earnings comparable to the particular occupation in the community where the veteran resides.

Marginal employment generally is deemed to exist when a veteran's earned income does not exceed the amount established by the U.S. Census Bureau as the poverty level for the veteran only. See the U.S. Census Bureau's poverty thresholds available here: **www.census.gov/hhes/www/poverty/data/threshld**. Special consideration will be given for veterans when the following criteria is met:

- The veteran is considered unemployable due to a service-connected disability(ies) but fails to meet the minimum percentage standards.

- There is evidence of exceptional or unusual circumstances to impairment of earning capacity due to disabilities (for example, interference with employment or frequent periods of hospitalization).

Veterans may have to complete an employment questionnaire once a year in order for VA to determine continued eligibility to individual unemployability.

Grants, Allowances, and Additional Payments

In addition to compensation, the VA offers several grant and allowance programs to help disabled veterans afford the tools and comforts that will allow them to cope with their disability. These allowances include money for housing adaptations, clothing, automobiles, etc.

Housing grants

Certain veterans and service members with service-connected disabilities may be entitled to one of the VA's housing grants to help build a specially adapted house or buy a house and modify it to meet their disability-related requirements. These grants are designed to help provide a barrier-free living environment that affords the individual a level of independent living they may not otherwise enjoy, such as creating a wheelchair-accessible home.

VA has three main grant programs to assist disabled veterans and service members with necessary home modifications.

Specially Adapted Housing (SAH) grant

Veterans and service members with specific service-connected disabilities may be entitled to this grant for the purpose of constructing or modifying a home to meet their adaptive needs. The grant currently is limited to $63,780.

The SAH grant is available to veterans and service members who will be entitled to disability compensation for permanent and total disability due to:

- Loss or loss of use of both lower extremities, such as to preclude locomotion without the aid of braces, crutches, canes, or a wheelchair
- Blindness in both eyes, having only light perception, plus loss or loss of use of one lower extremity
- Loss or loss of use of one lower extremity together with (1) residuals of organic disease or injury, or (2) the loss or loss of use of one upper extremity, which so affects the functions of balance

or propulsion as to preclude locomotion without the aid of braces, crutches, canes, or a wheelchair

- Loss or loss of use of both upper extremities such as to preclude use of the arms at or above the elbow
- A severe burn injury (as so determined)

For more information on the SAH grant, visit **www.benefits.va.gov/homeloans/docs/part1_va_pamphlet_26_jrd_edits_doc.pdf**.

Special Home Adaptation (SHA) grant

VA may approve a grant for the cost, up to a maximum of $12,756, for necessary adaptations to a veteran's or service member's residence or to help veterans and service-members acquire a residence already adapted with special features for their disability. To be eligible for this grant, veterans and service-members must be entitled to compensation for permanent and total service-connected disability due to:

- Blindness in both eyes with 5/200 visual acuity or less
- Anatomical loss or loss of use of both hands
- Severe burn injuries

You can apply for the SAH and SHA grants by completing VA Form 26-4555, Veterans Application in Acquiring Specially Adapted Housing or Special Home Adaptation Grant, and submitting it to your local VA regional office. For more information on the SHA grant, visit **www.benefits.va.gov/homeloans/docs/part2_va_pamphlet_26_jrd_edits_doc.pdf**.

Home Improvement and Structural Alterations (HISA) grant

Under the HISA program, veterans may receive assistance for any home improvement necessary for the continuation of treatment or for disability access to the home and essential lavatory and sanitary facilities. A HISA grant is available to veterans who have received a medical determination indicating that improvements and structural alterations are necessary or appropriate for the effective and economical treatment of their disability. A veteran may receive both a HISA grant and either a SHA or SAH grant.

The HISA program is available for both service-connected veterans and non-service-connected veterans.

- Home improvement benefits up to $6,800 may be provided for a:
  o Service-connected condition
  o Non-service-connected condition of a veteran rated 50 percent or more service-connected
- Home improvement benefits up to $2,000 may be provided to all other veterans registered in the VA health care system

You can apply for a HISA grant by completed VA Form 10-0103, Veterans Application for Assistance in Acquiring Home Improvement and Structural Alterations, and submitting it to your local VA medical center. For more information on obtaining a HISA grant, visit **www.prosthetics.va.gov/ HISA2.asp**.

Temporary Residence Adaptation (TRA) grants

The Temporary Residence Adaptation (TRA) grant program is available to veterans and service members who have been rated eligible for the Specially Adapted Housing section 2101 (a) (SAH) or the Special Home Adaptation section 2101(b) (SHA) grant on a one-time basis.

The TRA Grant is intended to assist an eligible veteran or service member adapt a family member's home to meet the veteran's or service members special needs.

Veterans and service members eligible for a TRA grant may use up to $14,000 of the maximum grant amount for a section 2101(a) SAH grant or up to $2,000 of the maximum amount for a section 2101(b) SHA grant.

Eligible veterans who temporarily are residing in a home owned by a family member also may receive assistance in the form of a grant to assist in adapting the family member's home to meet his or her special needs. Those eligible for a $50,000 total grant would be permitted to use up to $14,000, and those eligible for a $10,000 total grant would be permitted to use up to $2,000. However, the VA is not authorized to make such grants available to assist active duty personnel.

Specially Adapted Housing (SAH) grant amounts will remain unchanged in fiscal year 2012 from the fiscal year 2011 amounts.

For more information on the SAH grant program and eligibility criteria, please visit **www.benefits.va.gov/homeloans/sah.asp**.

Payment for adapting an automobile

Financial assistance, in the form of a grant, is available to purchase a new or used automobile (or other conveyance) to accommodate a veteran or service member with certain disabilities that resulted from an injury or disease incurred or aggravated during active military service. The grant also may be paid, if disabilities are a result of medical treatment, examination, vocational rehabilitation, or compensated work therapy provided by the VA.

Veterans and service members may be eligible for a one-time payment of not more than $18,900 toward the purchase of an automobile or other conveyance if they have service-connected loss or permanent loss of use of one or both hands or feet, permanent impairment of vision of both eyes to a certain degree, or ankylosis (immobility) of one or both knees or one or both hips.

They also may be eligible for adaptive equipment, and for repair, replacement, or reinstallation required because of disability or for the safe operation of a vehicle purchased with VA assistance. Adaptive equipment includes but is not limited to, power steering, power brakes, power windows, power seats, and special equipment necessary to assist the eligible person into and out of the vehicle. Contact should be made with your local VA medical center's prosthetic department before purchasing any equipment. The adaptive equipment grant may be paid more than once, and it may be paid to either the seller or the veteran.

The grant is paid directly to the seller of the automobile for the total price (up to $11,000) of the automobile. The veteran or service member may only receive the automobile grant once in his or her lifetime.

Apply for the automobile and/or the special adaptive equipment grant by completing VA Form 21-4502, Application for Automobile or Other Conveyance and Adaptive Equipment (**www.vba.va.gov/pubs/forms/VBA-21-4502-ARE.pdf**), and submitting it to your local VA regional office. The instructions on the VA Form 21-4502 contain a list of adaptive equipment that has been preapproved for particular disabilities.

After you complete and submit Section I of the application, VA will complete Section II and return the original to you. You are responsible for obtaining the invoice from the seller, updating Section III, and submitting the form to your local VA regional office for payment.

If you are entitled to adaptive equipment only (i.e., service connected for ankylosis of knees or hips) complete VA Form 10-1394, Application for Adaptive Equipment — Motor Vehicle, and submit it to your local VA medical center. Additionally, VA Form 10-1394 should be completed for approval of equipment not specified on the VA Form 21-4502.

Annual clothing allowance

Any veteran who is service-connected for a disability for which he or she uses prosthetic or orthopedic appliances may receive an annual clothing allowance.

The clothing allowance also is available to any veteran whose service-connected skin condition requires prescribed medication that irreparably damages his or her outer garments. To apply, contact the prosthetic representative at the nearest VA medical center.

Rehabilitation and Assistance Services

Besides monetary compensation, the VA also offers several programs and initiatives for veterans disabled over the course of their active duty. The remainder of the chapter will discuss these programs so you will know which areas of your life could be helped by VA benefits.

Vocational Rehabilitation and Employment program

Vocational Rehabilitation and Employment is a program whose primary function is to help veterans with service-connected disabilities become suitably employed, maintain employment, or achieve independence in daily living. Independent living services are also available for severely disabled veterans who are not currently ready to seek employment.

The program offers a number of services to help each eligible disabled veteran reach his or her rehabilitation goal. These services include vocational and personal counseling, education and training, financial aid, job assistance, and, if needed, medical and dental treatment. Services generally last up to 48 months or their part-time equivalent, but they can be extended in certain instances.

VA pays the cost of all approved training programs. Subsistence allowance also may be provided. Depending on an individual's needs, services provided by VA may include:

- An evaluation of interests, aptitudes, and abilities

- Assistance with writing a resume and other job seeking skills
- Assistance with obtaining and maintaining suitable employment
- Vocational counseling and planning
- On-the-job training and work-experience programs
- Training, such as certificate, two, or four-year college or technical programs
- Supportive rehabilitation services and counseling

To be eligible, a veteran must have a VA service-connected disability rated at least 20 percent with an employment handicap or rated 10 percent with a serious employment handicap and be discharged or released from military service under other than dishonorable conditions. Usually, you must first be awarded a monthly VA disability compensation payment; however, in some cases, you may be eligible if you are not getting VA compensation. For example, if you are awaiting discharge from the service because of a disability, you may be eligible for vocational rehabilitation.

Service members pending medical separation from active duty also may apply if they expect their disabilities to be rated at least 20 percent following their discharge.

Generally, veterans must complete a program within 12 years from their separation from military service or within 12 years from the date VA notifies them that they have a compensable service-connected disability.

Veterans training at the three-quarter or full-time rate may participate in VA's work-study program. Participants may provide VA outreach services, prepare and process VA paperwork, and work at a VA medical facility or perform other VA-approved activities. If you need training, VA will pay your training costs, such as tuition and fees, books, supplies, equipment, and, if needed, special services. While you are in training, VA also will pay you a monthly benefit to help with living expenses, called a subsistence allowance. A portion of the work-study allowance equal to 40 percent of the total may be paid in advance.

Subsistence allowance is paid at the following monthly rates (as of 2013) for training in an institution of higher learning.

Training Time	Veterans With No Dependents	Veterans With One Dependent	Veterans With Two Dependents	Additional Dependent
Full-time	$594.47	$737.39	$868.96	$63.34
¾-time	$446.67	$553.85	$649.68	$48.71
½-time	$298.88	$370.30	$435.27	$32.50

Subsistence allowance is paid at the following monthly rates for full-time training only in non-pay or nominal pay on-the-job training in a federal, state, local, or federally recognized Indian tribe agency; training in the home; and vocational training in a rehabilitation facility or sheltered workshop.

Training Time	Veterans With No Dependents	Veterans With One Dependent	Veterans With Two Dependents	Additional Dependent
Full-time	$594.47	$737.39	$868.96	$63.34

Subsistence allowance is paid at the following monthly rates for full-time training only in farm cooperative, apprenticeship, and other on-job training. Payments are variable, based on the wages received. The maximum rates are:

Training Time	Veterans With No Dependents	Veterans With One Dependent	Veterans With Two Dependents	Additional Dependent
Full-time	$594.47	$737.39	$868.96	$63.34

Subsistence allowance is paid at the following monthly rates for non-pay or nominal pay work experience in a federal, state, local, or federally recognized Indian tribe agency.

Training Time	Veterans With No Dependents	Veterans With One Dependent	Veterans With Two Dependents	Additional Dependent
Full-time	$594.47	$737.39	$868.96	$63.34
¾-time	$446.67	$553.85	$649.68	$48.71

Training Time	Veterans With No Dependents	Veterans With One Dependent	Veterans With Two Dependents	Additional Dependent
½-time	$298.88	$370.30	$435.27	$32.50

Subsistence allowance is paid at the following monthly rates for training programs that include a combination of institutional and on-job training.

Greater Than Half-Time	Veterans With No Dependents	Veterans With One Dependent	Veterans With Two Dependents	Additional Dependent
Institutional	$594.47	$737.39	$868.96	$63.34
On-job	$446.67	$553.85	$649.68	$48.71

Subsistence allowance is paid at the following monthly rates for full-time training only for non-farm cooperative institutional training and non-farm cooperative on-job training.

Training Time	Veterans With No Dependents	Veterans With One Dependent	Veterans With Two Dependents	Additional Dependent
Institutional	$594.47	$737.39	$868.96	$63.34
On-job	$446.67	$553.85	$649.68	$48.71

Subsistence allowance is paid at the following monthly rates during the period of enrollment in a rehabilitation facility when a veteran is pursuing an approved independent living program plan.

Training Time	Veterans With No Dependents	Veterans With One Dependent	Veterans With Two Dependents	Additional Dependent
Full-time	$594.47	$737.39	$868.96	$63.34
¾-time	$446.67	$553.85	$649.68	$48.71
½-time	$298.88	$370.30	$435.27	$32.50

Subsistence allowance is paid at the following monthly rates during the period of enrollment in a rehabilitation facility when a veteran requires this service for the purpose of extended evaluation.

Training Time	Veterans With No Dependents	Veterans With One Dependent	Veterans With Two Dependents	Additional Dependent
Full-time	$594.47	$737.39	$868.96	$63.34
¾-time	$446.67	$553.85	$649.68	$48.71
½-time	$298.88	$370.30	$435.27	$32.50

You can apply by filling out VA Form 28-1900, Disabled Veterans Application for Vocational Rehabilitation and mail it to the VA regional office that serves your area. You can also apply online at **http://vabenefits.vba.va.gov/vonapp**. Additional information is available at this site as well.

Disabled Transition Assistance Program (DTAP)

The Disabled Transition Assistance Program (DTAP) is an integral component of transition assistance that involves intervention on behalf of service members who may be released because of a disability or who believe they have a disability qualifying them for VA's Vocational Rehabilitation and Employment Program. DTAP's goal is to encourage and assist potentially eligible service members in making an informed decision about VA's Vocational Rehabilitation and Employment Program. It also is intended to facilitate the expeditious delivery of vocational rehabilitation services to eligible persons by assisting them in filing an application for vocational rehabilitation benefits.

DTAP presentations are generally group sessions that include a comprehensive discussion of VA's Vocational Rehabilitation and Employment Program and educational/vocational counseling available to separating service members and veterans. Usually, the VA Regional Office VR&E officer will coordinate DTAP sessions for service members who are hospitalized, convalescing, or receiving outpatient treatment for a disability and who are unable to attend a DTAP group session. DTAP sessions may include a review of a service member's medical records. A brief overview of the VR&E program is available online at **www.vba.va.gov/bln/vre**.

Chapter 8

Life Insurance Benefits During and After your Military Career

Every active duty military service member knows about SGLI coverage. Many do not know about family coverage, and even less know about VGLI, the Survivor Benefit Plan and other insurance options available to veterans or military retirees to help them ensure their families and debts are covered once they die. This chapter provides you with an in-depth explanation of costs, benefits, eligibility, and options for each.

Service Members' Group Life Insurance (SGLI)

SGLI is a program of low-cost group life insurance for service members on active duty, ready reservists, members of the National Guard, members of the Commissioned Corps of the National Oceanic and Atmospheric Administration and the Public Health Service, cadets and midshipmen of the four service academies, and members of the Reserve Officer Training Corps.

SGLI coverage is available in $50,000 increments up to a maximum of $400,000. The current SGLI premium rate is 6.5 cents per month per $1,000 of coverage, or $27 a month. The premium includes an additional $1 per month for Traumatic Injury Protection coverage (TSGLI), which is mandatory and added automatically. *TSGLI will be explained in more detail later in this chapter.*

Coverage Amount	Monthly Premium rate	TSGLI Premium	Total Monthly Premium Deduction
50,000	$3.25	$1.00	$4.25
100,000	$6.50	$1.00	$7.50
150,000	$9.75	$1.00	$10.75
200,000	$13.00	$1.00	$14.00
250,000	$16.25	$1.00	$17.25
300,000	$19.50	$1.00	$20.50
350,000	$22.75	$1.00	$23.75
400,000	$26.00	$1.00	$27.00

Service members with SGLI coverage have two options available to them upon release from service. They can convert their full-time SGLI coverage to term insurance under the Veterans' Group Life Insurance program or convert to a permanent plan of insurance with one of the participating commercial insurance companies.

The SGLI Disability Extension

The SGLI Disability Extension allows service members who are totally disabled at time of discharge to retain the service members' Group Life Insurance (SGLI) coverage they had in service at no cost for up to two years.

The SGLI Disability Extension is available to you if you are totally disabled at time of discharge. To be considered totally disabled, you must have a disability that prevents you from being gainfully employed or have one of the following conditions, regardless of your employment status:

- Permanent loss of use of both hands
- Permanent loss of use of both feet
- Permanent loss of use of both eyes
- Permanent loss of use of one hand and one foot
- Permanent loss of use of one foot and one eye

- Permanent loss of use of one hand and one eye
- Total loss of hearing in both ears
- Organic loss of speech (lost ability to express oneself, both by voice and whisper, through normal organs for speech — being able to speak with an artificial appliance is disregarded in determination of total disability)

Download VA form 8715, Application for SGLI Disability Extension to apply for this insurance. This form is available here: **www.insurance.va.gov/sglisite/ forms/8715(06-2011).pdf.**

Veterans Group Life Insurance (VGLI)

VGLI is a program of post-separation insurance that allows service members to convert their SGLI coverage to renewable term insurance. Members with full-time SGLI coverage are eligible for VGLI upon release from service.

VGLI premiums are based upon the separating member's age. Coverage is issued in multiples of $10,000 up to a maximum of $400,000. However, a service member's VGLI coverage amount cannot exceed the amount of SGLI he or she had in force at the time of separation from service.

To convert SGLI to VGLI, an eligible member must submit an SGLV 8714, Application for Veterans' Group Life Insurance, to the Office of Service members' Group Life Insurance with the required premium within one year and 120 days from discharge. However, service members who apply after the 120-day period must submit evidence of good health. Service members who submit their application within 120 days of discharge do not need to submit evidence of good health.

The VA can help you figure out how much insurance you need. To assess your life insurance needs, follow this link to the VA Insurance Needs Calculator: **www.insurance.va.gov/sglisite/calculator/LifeIns101.htm.**

VGLI policyholders can convert their VGLI to an individual commercial life insurance policy at any time. In order to convert VGLI coverage, the policyholder must:

- Select a company from the participating companies listing.
- Apply to a local sales office of the company selected.
- Obtain a letter from OSGLI verifying coverage (VGLI Conversion Notice).
- Give a copy of that notice to the agent who takes the application.

Policyholders may convert their coverage to a commercial policy at standard premium rates, without having to provide proof of good health. The conversion policy must be a permanent policy, such as a whole life policy.

Other types of policies, such as term, variable life, or universal life insurance are not allowed as conversion policies. In addition, supplementary policy benefits such as accidental death and dismemberment or waiver of premium for disability are not considered part of the conversion policy. A list of participating companies may be found here: **www.insurance. va.gov/sgliSite/forms/ParticList.htm**.

Veterans' Mortgage Life Insurance (VMLI)

The Veterans' Mortgage Life Insurance (VMLI) program provides mortgage life insurance to severely disabled veterans. It is designed to pay off home mortgages of disabled veterans in the event of their death.

Only veterans who have received a Specially Adapted Housing grant, discussed in Chapter 7, from VA are eligible for VMLI. Veterans who receive a grant for the purchase of Specially Adapted Housing are advised by Loan Guaranty personnel at their interview of their eligibility for life insurance to cover the unpaid mortgage on their home.

VMLI provides up to $90,000 mortgage life insurance payable to the mortgage holder (i.e., a bank or mortgage lender), in the event of the veteran's death. The amount of coverage will equal the amount of the mortgage still owed, but the maximum can never exceed $90,000. VMLI is decreasing term insurance that reduces as the amount of the mortgage reduced. VMLI has no loan or cash values and pays no dividends.

The VA has a premium calculator available to help you determine your VMLI premium amount, which is available here: **https://insurance.va.gov/VMLICalc/VMLICalc.asp**.

You can get more information about VMLI by downloading and viewing the VMLI Brochure from **www.va.gov**. The application for VMLI, VA Form 29-8636, Application for Veterans' Mortgage Life Insurance is also available for download from this site.

Service-Disabled Veterans Insurance (S-DVI)

The Service-Disabled Veterans Insurance (S-DVI) program was established to meet the insurance needs of certain veterans with service connected disabilities. S-DVI is available in a variety of permanent plans and term insurance. Policies are issued for a maximum face amount of $10,000.

You can apply for S-DVI if you meet the following four criteria:

- You were released from active duty under other than dishonorable conditions on or after April 25, 1951.
- You were rated for a service-connected disability (even if only 0 percent).
- You are in good health except for any service-connected conditions.
- You apply within two years from the date VA grants your new service-connected disability.

An increase in an existing service-connected disability or the granting of individual unemployability of a previous rated condition does not entitle a veteran to this insurance.

Under certain conditions, the basic S-DVI policy provides for a waiver of premiums in case of total disability. Policyholders who carry the basic

S-DVI coverage and who become eligible for a waiver of premiums due to total disability can apply for and be granted additional Supplemental S-DVI of up to $20,000.

You can apply online at **www.va.gov** or download VA form 29-4364, Application for Service-Disabled Veterans Life Insurance. Also, be sure to download VA Pamphlet 29-9 from this site for premiums rates and a description of the plans available.

Supplemental S-DVI

The Veterans' Benefits Act of 1992 provided for $20,000 of supplemental coverage to S-DVI policyholders. Premiums may not be waived on this supplemental coverage. S-DVI policyholders are eligible for this supplemental coverage if:

- They are eligible for a waiver of premiums.
- They apply for the coverage within one year from notice of the grant of waiver.
- They are under age 65.

Traumatic Injury Protection Under SGLI (TSGLI)

Every member who has SGLI also has TSGLI. This coverage applies to active duty members, reservists, National Guard members, funeral honors duty, and one-day muster duty.

This benefit is also provided retroactively for members who incurred severe losses as a result of traumatic a injury between October 7, 2001, and December 1, 2005, if the loss was the direct result of injuries incurred in Operations Enduring Freedom or Iraqi Freedom.

TSGLI coverage will pay a benefit of between $25,000 and $100,000 depending on the loss directly resulting from the traumatic injury.

The following chart lists the loss to service member as well as how much they could receive for each injury.

PART I		
	Loss	**Payment Amount**
1.	**Sight:** total and permanent loss of sight or loss of sight that has lasted 120 days • For each eye	$50,000
2.	**Hearing:** total and permanent loss of hearing • For one ear • For both ears	 $25,000 $100,000
3.	**Speech:** total and permanent loss of speech	$50,000
4.	**Quadriplegia:** complete paralysis of all four limbs	$100,000
5.	**Hemiplegia:** complete paralysis of the upper and lower limbs on one side of the body	$100,000
6.	**Paraplegia:** complete paralysis of both lower limbs	$100,000
7.	**Uniplegia:** complete paralysis of one limb* *Note: Payment for uniplegia of arm cannot be combined with loss 9, 10, or 14 for the same arm. Payment for uniplegia of leg cannot be combined with loss 11, 12, 13, or 15 for the same leg.	$50,000
8.	**Burns:** Second degree or worse burns to at least 20 percent of the body including the face or at least 20 percent of the face	$100,000
9.	**Amputation of hand:** amputation at or above the wrist • For each hand* *Note: Payment for loss 9 cannot be combined with payment for loss 10 for the same hand.	 $50,000
10.	**Amputation of four fingers on one hand OR thumb alone:** amputation at or above the metacarpophalangeal joint • For each hand	 $50,000
11.	**Amputation of foot:** amputation at or above the ankle • For each foot* *Note: Payment for loss 11 cannot be combined with payments for losses 12 or 13 for the same foot.	 $50,000
12.	**Amputation of all toes including the big toe on one foot:** amputation at or above the metatarsophalangeal joint • For each foot *Note: Payment for loss 12 cannot be combined with payments for loss 13 for the same foot.	 $50,000

	Loss	Payment Amount
13.	**Amputation of big toe only, OR other four toes on one foot:** amputation at or above the metatarsophalangeal joint	
	• For each foot	$25,000
14.	**Limb salvage of arm:** salvage of arm in place of amputation	
	• For each arm*	$50,000
	*Note: Payment for loss 14 cannot be combined with payments for losses 9 or 10 for the same arm.	
15.	**Limb salvage of leg:** salvage of leg in place of amputation	
	• For each leg	$50,000
	*Note: Payment for loss 15 cannot be combined with payments for losses 11, 12, or 13 for the same leg.	
16.	**Facial Reconstruction:** reconstructive surgery to correct traumatic avulsions of the face or jaw that cause discontinuity defects.	
	• **Jaw:** surgery to correct discontinuity loss of the upper or lower jaw	$75,000
	• **Nose:** surgery to correct discontinuity loss of 50 percent or more of the cartilaginous nose	$50,000
	• **Lips:** surgery to correct discontinuity loss of 50 percent or more of the upper or lower lip	
	o For one lip	$50,000
	o For both lips	$75,000
	• **Eyes:** surgery to correct discontinuity loss of 30 percent or more of the periorbita	
	o For each eyep	$25,000
	• **Facial Tissue:** surgery to correct discontinuity loss of the tissue in 50 percent or more of any of the following facial subunits: forehead, temple, zygomatic, mandibular, infraorbital, or chin.	
	o For each facial subunit	$25,000
	Note 1: Injuries listed under facial reconstruction may be combined with each other, but the maximum benefit for facial reconstruction may not exceed $75,000.	
	Note 2: Any injury or combination of injuries under facial reconstruction may also be combined with other injuries listed in Part I and treated as one loss, provided that all injuries are the result of a single traumatic event. However, the total payment amount may not exceed $100,000.	

	Loss	Payment Amount
17.	**Coma from traumatic injury AND/OR Traumatic Brain Injury resulting in inability to perform at least two Activities of Daily Living (ADL)**	
	• At 15th consecutive day of coma or ADL loss	$25,000
	• At 30th consecutive day of coma or ADL loss	an additional $25,000
	• At 60th consecutive day of coma or ADL loss	an additional $25,000
	• At 90th consecutive day of coma or ADL loss	an additional $25,000
18.	**Hospitalization due to traumatic brain injury**	
	• At 15th consecutive day of hospitalization	$25,000
	Note 1: Payment for hospitalization replaces the first payment period in loss 17.	
	Note 2: Duration of hospitalization includes dates on which member is transported from the injury site to a facility described in § 9.20(e)(6)(xiii), admitted to the facility, transferred between facilities, and discharged from the facility.	
19.	**Traumatic injury resulting in inability to perform at least two Activities of Daily Living (ADL)**	
	• At 30th consecutive day of ADL loss	$25,000
	• At 60th consecutive day of ADL loss	an additional $25,000
	• At 90th consecutive day of ADL loss	an additional $25,000
	• At 120th consecutive day of ADL loss	an additional $25,000
20.	**Hospitalization due to traumatic injury**	
	• At 15th consecutive day of hospitalization	$25,000
	Note 1: Payment for hospitalization replaces the first payment period in loss 19.	
	Note 2: Duration of hospitalization includes dates on which member is transported from the injury site to a facility described in § 9.20(e)(6)(xiii), admitted to the facility, transferred between facilities, and discharged from the facility.	

For losses such as coma or traumatic brain injury, the TSGLI benefit is payable in $25,000 increments on the 15th, 30th, 60th, and 90th consecutive days of the member's inability to carry out activities of daily living. A separate claim for TSGLI must be filed at each time interval. For example, if a service member suffers a traumatic injury that leaves him in a coma, a claim for TSGLI should be filed after the 15th consecutive day of the member being in a coma for which $25,000 is payable. If the member remains in a coma for 30 days after the traumatic injury, another claim should be submitted, and another $25,000 will be paid.

If a member files a claim for an incurred loss and then subsequently incurs another loss because of the same traumatic event, a new claim must be filed for the subsequent loss. For example, if a member files a claim for losing one leg because of an explosion and four months later, has the other leg amputated because of that same explosion, the member must file another claim for the loss of the leg.

Costs of TSGLI

The premium for TSGLI is a flat rate of $1 per month for most service members. Members who carry the maximum SGLI coverage of $400,000 will pay $27.00 per month for both SGLI and TSGLI.

The table below outlines the rates for various categories of SGLI coverage.

Duty Status	Premium
Active duty members	$1 per month
Reservists or National Guard members w/full-time coverage	$1 per month
Reservists or National Guard members w/part-time coverage	$1 per year
Funeral honors & 1 day muster duty	No charge

TSGLI eligibility and claims

To be eligible for payment of TSGLI, you must meet all of the following requirements:

- If injured on or after December 1, 2005, you must be insured by SGLI when you experience a traumatic event. For those injured between October 7, 2001, and November 30, 2005, SGLI coverage is not required to be eligible for TSGLI.

- You must incur a scheduled loss, and that loss must be a direct result of a traumatic injury.

- You must have suffered the traumatic injury before midnight of the day that you separate from the uniformed services.

- You must suffer a scheduled loss within two years (730 days) of the traumatic injury.

- You must survive for a period of not less than seven full days from the date of the traumatic injury. (The seven-day period begins on the date and time of the traumatic injury, as measured by Zulu [Greenwich Meridian] time and ends 168 full hours later).

As long as the service member experienced the traumatic event while in service and covered by SGLI, he or she can apply for the benefit even if he or she has since been discharged.

In order to make a claim for the TSGLI benefit, the member (or someone acting on his or her behalf) should download the SGLV-8600, Application for TSGLI Benefits. You also can obtain this form from your service department point of contact or from the Office of Servicemembers' Group Life Insurance by email at **osgli.claims@prudential.com**.

The TSGLI Application has two parts:

- Part A is to be completed by the service member or, if incapacitated, by the member's guardian or the member's attorney-in-fact.
- Part B is to be completed by the attending medical professional.

Once both parts of the application are completed, the application should be sent to the appropriate branch of service TSGLI office listed on the first page of the application.

Payment of TSGLI benefits

The service member is the beneficiary of TSGLI. The member cannot name someone other than himself or herself as the TSGLI beneficiary. If the member is incompetent, the benefit will be paid to his or her guardian or attorney-in-fact.

If the service member dies as a result of the traumatic injury, TSGLI is still payable if the member survived for a period of not less than seven full days from the date of the traumatic event and died before the maximum benefit for which the service member qualifies is paid.

Payment of TSGLI has no impact on the amount of SGLI payable. For example, if a service member is insured for $400,000 of SGLI coverage and receives a TSGLI payment of $50,000 for a traumatic injury, that member is still insured for the full $400,000 of SGLI coverage, which will be paid upon the service member's death. If the service member is deceased, the TSGLI payment will be made to the beneficiary or beneficiaries of the member's basic SGLI.

TSGLI payments will be made by one of the following methods:

- **Electronic Funds Transfer (EFT)** — Under this option, the TSGLI payment is credited electronically to the bank account specified by the service member. This option is available to the service member, the member's guardian, or power of attorney.

- **Prudential's Alliance Account** — An Alliance Account is an interest-bearing draft account established in the member's name with a draft book. The member can write drafts (checks) for any amount up to the full amount of the proceeds. This gives the member time to make important financial decisions while his or her funds are secure and earning continuous interest. There are no monthly service fees or per check charges, and additional checks can be ordered at no cost, but fees apply for some special services including returned checks, stop payment orders, and copies of statements/checks.

- **Check** — Under this option, the service member's guardian or attorney-in-fact will receive a single check on behalf of the service member for the full TSGLI benefit payable. This option is available only to the service member's guardian or power of attorney.

The member may use his or her TSGLI benefit payment or payments in any manner. TSGLI benefit recipients may take advantage of the Beneficiary Financial Counseling Services (BFCS) program, which is the same no-cost counseling service to which SGLI or VGLI beneficiaries have access.

Chapter 9

Veterans Home Loan Program

A home loan guaranties are issued to help eligible service members, veterans, reservists, and unmarried surviving spouses obtain homes, condominiums, residential cooperative housing units, and manufactured homes, and to refinance loans. For additional information or to obtain VA loan guaranty forms, visit **www. homeloans.va.gov**.

What a VA Loan Does

A VA guaranty helps protect lenders from loss if the borrower fails to repay the loan. It can be used to obtain a loan to:

- Buy or build a home
- Buy a residential condominium unit
- Buy a residential cooperative housing unit
- Repair, alter, or improve a residence owned by the veteran and occupied as a home
- Refinance an existing home loan
- Buy a manufactured home and/or lot
- Install a solar heating or cooling system or other energy-efficient improvements

VA guaranty amount varies with the size of the loan and the location of the property. VA will guarantee 25 percent of the principal loan amount up to the maximum guaranty, which varies depending upon the location of the property.

For all locations in the United States other than Alaska, Guam, Hawaii, and the U.S. Virgin Islands, the maximum guaranty is the greater of 25 percent of (a) $417,000 or (b) 125 percent of the area median price for a single-family residence, but in no case will the guaranty exceed 175 percent of the loan limit for a single-family residence in the county in which the property securing the loan is located.

In Alaska, Guam, Hawaii, and the U.S. Virgin Islands, the maximum guaranty is the greater of 25 percent of (a) $625,500 or (b) 125 percent of the area median price for a single-family residence, but in no case will the guaranty exceed 175 percent of the loan limit for a single-family residence in the county in which the property securing the loan is located.

A list of 2014 county loan limits can be found at the following website: **www.benefits.va.gov/HOMELOANS/loan_limits.asp.** The VA funding fee and up to $6,000 of energy-efficient improvements can be included in VA loans. The veteran must pay other closing costs, except on refinancing loans where most costs can be included in the loan.

The VA Home Loan Program is designed to streamline the process for you to get a home loan. Typically, VA loans are made without any down payments and may offer lower interest rates than ordinarily available with other types of loans. Aside from the veteran's certificate of eligibility and the VA-assigned appraisal, the application process is almost identical to any other mortgage loan.

If a lender is approved under VA's Lender Appraisal Processing Program (LAPP), the lender may review the appraisal completed by a VA-assigned appraiser and close the loan based on that review. The overall process can be quick and efficient.

VA appraises the house to determine its reasonable value in the housing market at the time the appraisal is made. VA requires compliance inspections in most cases on proposed new construction to see that the house meets accepted standards of good construction and conforms to the plans and specifications on which VA's appraisal is based. VA will try to assist you in getting your builder to correct any defects about which you may have valid complaints.

An eligible borrower can use a VA-guaranteed Interest Rate Reduction Refinancing Loan to refinance an existing VA loan to lower the interest rate and payment. Typically, no credit underwriting is required for this type of loan. The loan may include the entire outstanding balance of the prior loan, the costs of energy-efficient improvements, as well as closing costs, including up to two discount points.

For purchase home loans, payment in cash is required on all closing costs, including title search and recording fees, hazard insurance premiums, and prepaid taxes. For refinancing loans, all such costs may be included in the loan as long as the total loan does not exceed the reasonable value of the property.

All veterans, except those receiving VA disability compensation, those who are rated by VA as eligible to receive compensation because of predischarge disability examination and rating, and unmarried surviving spouses of veterans who died in service or because of a service-connected disability, are charged a VA funding fee. For all types of loans, the loan amount may include this funding fee.

Financing, Interest Rates, and Terms

Veterans obtain VA guaranteed loans through the usual lending institutions, including banks, credit unions, and mortgage brokers. VA-guaranteed loans can have either a fixed interest rate or an adjustable rate, in which the interest rate may adjust up to 1 percent annually and up to 5 percent over the life of the loan. VA does not set the interest rate. Interest rates are negotiable between the lender and borrower on all loan types.

Veterans also may choose a different type of adjustable rate mortgage called a hybrid ARM, in which the initial interest rate remains fixed for three to ten years. If the rate remains fixed for less than five years, the rate adjustment cannot be more than 1 percent annually and 5 percent over the life of the loan. For a hybrid ARM with an initial fixed period of five years or more, the initial adjustment may be up to 2 percent. Currently, annual adjustments may be up to 2 percentage points and 6 percent over the life of the loan. If the lender charges discount points on the loan, the veteran may negotiate with the seller as to who will pay points or if they will be split between buyer and seller. Points paid by the veteran may not be included in the loan (with the exception that up to two points may be included in interest rate reduction refinancing loans). The term of the loan may be for as long as 30 years and 32 days.

What the VA does not do

VA does not have the legal authority to act as your architect. It does not supervise construction of the house you buy. The VA does not guarantee that the house is free of defects. And the VA cannot act as your attorney.

It cannot provide you legal services if you run into trouble in buying or constructing your home.

The VA cannot compel a builder to remedy defects in construction or otherwise compel the builder to live up to a contract with you. The VA cannot guarantee that you will be satisfied completely with the house or that you can resell it at the price you paid. The VA cannot guarantee that you are making a good investment. That is a decision only you can make. The VA does not guarantee the condition of the house you are buying, whether it is new or previously occupied. VA guarantees only the loan.

You may talk to many people when you are in the process of buying a house. Particularly with a previously occupied house, you may pick up the impression along the way that you need not be overly concerned about any needed repairs or hidden defects because VA will be sure to find them and require them to be repaired. This is not true. In every case, ultimately, it is your responsibility to be an informed buyer and to assure yourself that what you are buying is satisfactory in all respects. Remember, VA guarantees only the loan, not the condition of the house.

If you have any doubts about the condition of the house you are buying, it is in your best interest to seek expert advice before you commit yourself legally in a purchase agreement. Particularly with a previously occupied house, most sellers and their real estate agents are willing to permit you, at your expense, to arrange for an inspection by a qualified residential inspection service. Also, most sellers and agents are willing to negotiate with you concerning what repairs are to be included in the purchase agreement. Steps of this kind can prevent many later problems, disagreements, and major disappointments.

General Rules for VA Home Loan Eligibility

To qualify for a VA home loan, a veteran or the spouse of an active duty service member must certify that he or she intends to occupy the home. When refinancing a VA-guaranteed loan solely to reduce the interest rate, a veteran need only certify prior occupancy.

Military service requirements

To qualify for a home loan from the VA, you will need to have served during one of the combat periods specified in Chapter 1 of this book. Therefore, if you fought during World War II, during the post-World War II period, the Korean War, the post-Korean War period, the Vietnam War, the post-Vietnam period, or the Gulf War, you are eligible. *Refer back to Chapter 1 for specific dates defining these periods.*

You also could be eligible under the 24-Month Rule. If your service was between September 8, 1980, (October 16, 1981, for officers) and August 1, 1990, you must complete 24 months of continuous active duty service or the full period (at least 181 days) for which you were called or ordered to active duty, and be discharged under conditions other than dishonorable.

Exceptions are allowed if the veteran completed at least 181 days of active duty service but was discharged earlier than 24 months for (1) hardship, (2) the convenience of the government, (3) reduction-in-force, (4) certain medical conditions, or (5) service-connected disability. Applications involving other than honorable discharges usually will require further development by VA.

Selected Reserves or National Guard

If you are not otherwise eligible and you have completed a total of six years in the Selected Reserves or National Guard (member of an active unit, attended required weekend drills, and two-week active duty for training), you also might be eligible if you have the following requirements:

- Were discharged with an honorable discharge
- Were placed on the retired list
- Were transferred to the Standby Reserve or an element of the Ready Reserve other than the Selected Reserve after service characterized as honorable service
- Continue to serve in the Selected Reserves

Individuals who completed less than six years may be eligible if discharged for a service-connected disability.

Eligibility also may be established for:

- Certain United States citizens who served in the armed forces of a government allied with the United States in World War II

- Individuals with service as members in certain organizations, such as Public Health Service officers, cadets at the United States Military, Air Force, or Coast Guard Academies, midshipmen at the United States Naval Academy, officers of National Oceanic & Atmospheric Administration, merchant seaman with World War II service, and others

How do I prove I am eligible?

You will need a Certificate of Eligibility (COE) before you can get a VA-backed loan. Category A: veterans, active duty, and reservists/National Guard members who have served on active duty and Category B: reservists/National Guard members who have never served on active duty can get a Certificate of Eligibility (COE) in any of three ways:

1. **Apply online.** Go to the eBenefits portal (**www.ebenefits.va.gov**) and click on the My eBenefits tab towards the top, on the left side. It will open a screen with several benefit areas. On the bottom right of the screen is the Housing tab. You will need login credentials to request a Certificate of Eligibility (COE). If you have them, enter your username and password. If you need to request login credentials, you can simply click on the "Request/Activate a DoD Self-Service Logon" link, which is shown below the area where you logon.

2. **Apply through the lender.** In many cases, lenders can obtain a certificate online in minutes.

3. **Apply by mail.** Use VA Form 26-1880 (**www.vba.va.gov/pubs/forms/vba-26-1880-are.pdf**). Return it to the address shown on the form.

Category C: Surviving spouses of veterans who died in service or because of service must apply for the certificate by mail.

If your veteran spouse died after service, VA must determine that the death was due to a service-connected disability. Please allow two to three months for this process unless you know that the decision on service-connected death has already been made.

What evidence will I need to get the certificate?

The evidence you need depends on the nature of your eligibility. This chart explains.

If you are. . .	You should submit . . .
Veteran (Includes a member or former member of the National Guard or Reserves who was once activated for federal service)	DD Form 214. You are required to submit a copy showing the character of service (item 24) and the narrative reason for separation (item 28).
A discharged member of the National Guard who has never been activated for federal service	Either: NGB Form 22, Report of Separation and Record of Service, for each period of National Guard service or NGB Form 23, Retirement Points Accounting, and proof of the character of service
A discharged member of the Selected Reserve who has never been acti-vated for federal service	Copy of your latest annual retirement points statement and evidence of honorable service

If you are. . .	You should submit . . .
The surviving spouse of a service member who died on active duty	If you are already receiving Dependency and Indemnity Compensation (DIC), you do not need to send any documents. If you do not receive DIC, please send us • A copy of the DD Form 1300 (Report of Casualty) from the military • A copy of your marriage certificate It would be a good idea to add a simple signed statement saying that you would like to apply for DIC. If you qualify for the home loan benefit, you probably qualify for monthly payments under DIC. Put the service member's Social Security number on all documents.
The surviving spouse of a veteran who died because of military service	If you are already receiving Dependency and Indemnity Compensation (DIC), send us a copy of your award letter. (Generally, you already will have a record on file at a VA regional benefits office.) If you do not receive Dependency and Indemnity Compensation (DIC), please send us • A copy of the veteran's DD Form 214 • A copy of the veteran's death certificate • A copy of your marriage certificate

Regional loan centers

Regional Loan Center	Jurisdiction	Mailing and Website Addresses	Telephone Number
Atlanta	Georgia North Carolina South Carolina Tennessee	Department of Veterans Affairs Regional Loan Center 1700 Clairmont Rd. PO Box 100026 Decatur, GA 30031-7026 **www2.va.gov/directory/guide/facility. asp?ID=357&dnum=All**	800-827-1000
Cleveland	Delaware Indiana Michigan New Jersey Ohio Pennsylvania	Department of Veterans Affairs Cleveland Regional Loan Center 1240 East Ninth Street Cleveland, OH 44199 **www.vba.va.gov/ro/central/cleve/ index1.htm**	800-729-5772

Regional Loan Center	Jurisdiction	Mailing and Website Addresses	Telephone Number
Denver	Alaska Colorado Idaho Montana Oregon Utah Washington Wyoming	Department of Veterans Affairs VA Regional Loan Center Box 25126 Denver, CO 80225 **www.vba.va.gov/ro/denver/loan/lgy. htm**	888-349-7541
Honolulu	Hawaii	Department of Veterans Affairs Loan Guaranty Division (26) 459 Patterson Rd. Honolulu, HI 96819 *Although not an RLC, this office is a fully functioning Loan Guaranty operation for Hawaii.	808-433-0481
Houston	Arkansas Louisiana Oklahoma Texas	Department of Veterans Affairs VA Regional Loan Center 6900 Almeda Road Houston, TX 77030 **www.vba.va.gov/ro/houston/index.htm**	800-827-1000
Manchester	Connecticut Massachusetts Maine New Hampshire New York Rhode Island Vermont	Department of Veterans Affairs VA Regional Loan Center 275 Chestnut Street Manchester, NH 03101 **www.vba.va.gov/ro/manchester/lgy-main/loans.html**	800-827-6311 800-827-0336
Phoenix	Arizona California New Mexico Nevada	Department of Veterans Affairs VA Regional Loan Center 3333 N. Central Avenue Phoenix, AZ 85012-2402 **www2.va.gov/directory/guide/facility. asp?ID=1053&dnum=3**	800-827-1000
Roanoke	District of Columbia Kentucky Maryland Virginia West Virginia	Department of Veterans Affairs Roanoke Regional Loan Center 116 N. Jefferson Street Roanoke, VA 24016 **www.vba.va.gov/ro/roanoke/rlc**	800-827-0336

Regional Loan Center	Jurisdiction	Mailing and Website Addresses	Telephone Number
St. Paul	Illinois Iowa Kansas Minnesota Missouri Nebraska North Dakota South Dakota Wisconsin	Department of Veterans Affairs VA Regional Loan Center 1 Federal Drive Fort Snelling St. Paul, MN 55111-4050 **www.vba.va.gov/ro/central/stpau/ pages/homeloans.html**	800-827- 1000
St. Petersburg	Alabama Florida Mississippi Puerto Rico U.S. Virgin Islands	Department of Veterans Affairs VA Regional Loan Center PO Box 1437 St. Petersburg, FL 33731-1437 **www.vba.va.gov/ro/south/spete/rlc/ index.htm**	888-611-5916 (out of state) 800-827-1000 (in FL)

Interest Rate Reduction Refinancing Loan (IRRRL)

Sometimes you require additional cash now, for a real need. Perhaps you need to pay college tuition, or perhaps it is time to make improvements that will increase the value of your home before sale. Maybe you just want to take advantage of lower interest rates so you can keep more of your hard-earned money in your own pocket. An Interest Rate Reduction Loan or Streamline Refinance allows you to refinance your current mortgage interest rate to a lower rate than you are currently paying. This is only available to veterans who are refinancing their original VA mortgage and utilized their original eligibility.

"No cost" streamlines let you refinance your mortgage with no out-of-pocket expenses. One option is to let the lender pay the costs in exchange for a higher interest rate. Another option that lets you obtain market rates is to roll the closing costs into the new loan.

No lender is required to make you an IRRRL. However, any lender of your choice may process your application. Although it might be the best place to start shopping for an IRRRL, you do not have to go to the lender you make your payments to now or to the lender from whom you originally obtained your VA Loan. Veterans strongly are urged to contact several lenders. There may be big differences in the terms offered by the various lenders you contact. The only cost required by VA is a funding fee of half of 1 percent of the loan amount that may be paid in cash or included in the loan. You must NOT receive any cash from the loan proceeds.

An IRRRL can be done only if you already have used your eligibility for a VA loan on the property you intend to refinance. It must be a VA-to-VA refinance, and it will reuse the entitlement you originally used. You may have used your entitlement by obtaining a VA loan when you bought your house, or by substituting your eligibility for that of the seller, if you assumed the loan. If you have your Certificate of Eligibility, take it to the lender to show the prior use of your entitlement.

Adding all of these items into your loan may result in a situation in which you owe more than the fair market value of the house and will reduce the benefit of refinancing because your payment will not be lowered as much as it could be. Also, you could have difficulty selling the house for enough to pay off your loan balance.

Some lenders offer IRRRLs as an opportunity to reduce the term of your loan from 30 years to 15 years. Although this can save you a lot of money in interest over the life of the loan, if the reduction in the interest rate is not at least one percent (two percent is better) and lots of new loan costs are rolled into the new loan, you may see a very large increase in your monthly payment. No loan other than the existing VA loan may be paid from the proceeds of an IRRRL. If you have a second mortgage, the holder must agree to subordinate that lien so that your new VA loan will be a first mortgage.

For more information, visit **www.valoans.com/va_refinance.cfm**.

Chapter 10

Veteran Scholarships, Grants, and Aid

eterans enjoy a multitude of benefits in return for their service to our country. An outstanding benefit is eligibility of the veteran and their family members for a wide variety of scholarships, grants, and other programs to support them in their educational and employment funding. Corporations, organizations, the government, colleges, institutions, states, and more sponsor hundreds of programs. This chapter will cover several of them to get you started. You will find that most scholarships are geared toward high school age dependents of active duty military, and many others are for dependents of veterans. However, there are many for you as the veteran, if you know where to look. This list is certainly not all-inclusive, and discovering some of them may take some detective work on your part. You will find that in addition to the wealth of information provided by the VA, each state has significant veterans' benefits available. A search of your state's website will reveal many benefits, which are either federally or state funded, you may be entitled to. For example, the state of Florida publishes their veterans' benefits information at **www.floridavets. org/benefits/benefits.asp**.

Included are some national scholarships. The majority of the scholarships (and grants) are at the college or university level. You will need to visit your specific university's website for veterans' preference, benefits, scholarships, and grants to verify what each school offers for your specific situation.

Scholarship and Grant Programs for Dependents of Veterans

A Google™ search will review dozens of program you can apply for. Do some research online, as new scholarship and grant programs are routinely available. But here is a small sample of some of the opportunities available for veterans and their dependents.

The MG James Ursano Scholarship Program

This scholarship is for dependent children of soldiers on federal active duty, retired soldiers, or soldiers deceased while in active or retired status.

The MG James Ursano Scholarship Program offers scholarships based on financial need, academics, and leadership/achievement.

To be eligible, applicants must:

- Maintain a cumulative GPA of a 2.0 on a 4.0 scale
- Be full-time undergraduate students for the entire academic year at a school accredited by the U.S. Department of Education
- Be dependents of a soldier on federal active duty, a retiree, or a deceased active or retired soldier

To be a dependent you must be:

- Under the age of 23 for the entire academic year
- Registered in DEERS
- Unmarried for the entire academic year

The scholarship funds are split evenly between the fall and spring semesters, or terms or quarters. The funds are to be used for tuition, fees, books, supplies, and room and board either on or off campus as requested by the student. Applications are available at **www.aerhq.org**.

Dependents of deceased service members scholarship programs

The Navy-Marine Corps Relief Society provides educational assistance to the children and unremarried spouses of deceased service members. NMCRS Headquarters Education Division determines the awards.

You qualify for this scholarship if you are the dependent of a service member who died in retired status who died on active duty.

Some of the possible scholarships include:

- USS STARK Memorial Scholarship Fund: for dependent children of the crew members of the USS Stark who died, or were disabled, as a result of the missile attack on the ship in the Persian Gulf on May 17, 1987

- USS COLE Memorial Fund: for dependent children of crew members of the USS Cole who perished as a result of the terrorist attack of October 12, 2000

- Pentagon Assistance Fund: for dependent children of deceased military personnel who perished as a result of the terrorist attack on September 11, 2001

The application package and submission procedures may be found here: **www.nmcrs.org/child-dec.html**.

Federal Pell Grants

A Pell Grant provides eligible undergraduate students that have not earned a bachelor's degree or a professional degree a grant that does not require repayment. A student enrolled in a postbaccalaureate teacher certification program also may qualify.

The maximum Pell Grant for the 2013-14 award year (July 1, 2013 to June 30, 2014) was $5,645. The amount depends on your financial need, costs to attend school, status as a full-time or part-time student, and plans to attend school for a full academic year or less.

The maximum award amount is given for any Pell Grant eligible student whose parent or guardian died as a result of military service in Iraq or Afghanistan after September 11, 2001. You must be under 24 years old or enrolled at least part-time in college at the time of your parent or guardian's death. Beginning with the 2011-12 award year, you may receive only one Pell Grant award during a single award year.

Your school can apply Pell Grant funds to your school costs, pay you directly (usually by check), or combine these methods. The school must tell you in writing how much your award will be and how and when you will be paid. Schools must disburse funds at least once per term (semester, trimester, or quarter). Schools that do not use semesters, trimesters, or quarters must disburse funds at least twice per academic year.

For more information about or to apply for a Pell Grant, visit **www.ed.gov/programs/fpg/index.html**.

Survivors & Dependents Assistance (DEA)

Dependents' Educational Assistance provides education and training opportunities to eligible dependents of certain veterans. The program offers up to 45 months of education benefits. These benefits may be used for degree and certificate programs, apprenticeships, and on-the-job training. If you are a spouse, you may take a correspondence course. Remedial, deficiency, and refresher courses may be approved under certain circumstances.

To be eligible, you must be the son, daughter, or spouse of:

- A veteran who died or is permanently and totally disabled as the result of a service-connected disability. The disability must arise out of active service in the Armed Forces.

- A veteran who died from any cause while such permanent and total service-connected disability was in existence

- A service member missing in action or captured in line of duty by a hostile force

- A service member forcibly detained or interned in line of duty by a foreign government or power

- A service member who is hospitalized or receiving outpatient treatment for a service-connected permanent and total disability and is likely to be discharged for that disability

If you are a son or daughter and wish to receive benefits for attending school or job training, you must be between the ages of 18 and 26. In certain instances, it is possible to begin before age 18 and to continue after age 26. Marriage is not a bar to this benefit. If you are in the Armed Forces, you may not receive this benefit while on active duty. To pursue training after military service, your discharge must not be under dishonorable conditions. VA can extend your period of eligibility by the number of months and days equal to the time spent on active duty. Although this extension generally cannot go beyond your 31st birthday, there are some exceptions.

If you are a spouse, benefits end ten years from the date VA finds you eligible or from the date of death of the veteran. If the VA rated the veteran permanently and totally disabled with an effective date of three years from discharge, a spouse will remain eligible for 20 years from the effective date of the rating. For surviving spouses (spouses of service members who died on active duty), benefits end 20 years from the date of death.

How to apply

Make sure your selected program is approved for VA training. If you are not clear on this point, VA will inform you and the school or company about the requirements.

Obtain and complete VA Form 22-5490, Application for Survivors' and Dependents' Educational Assistance. Send it to the VA regional office with jurisdiction over the state where you will train. If you are a son or daughter, under legal age, a parent or guardian must sign the application.

If you have started training, take your application to your school or employer. Ask them to complete VA Form 22-1999, Enrollment Certification, and send both forms to the VA.

Special Restorative Training is available to persons eligible for DEA benefits. The VA may prescribe this training when needed to overcome or lessen the effects of a physical or mental disability so an eligible person can pursue an educational program, a special vocational program, or another appropriate goal. Medical care and treatment and psychiatric treatments are not included.

Special Vocational Training is also available to persons eligible for DEA benefits. This type of program may be approved for an eligible person who is not in need of Special Restorative Training but who requires a vocational program because of a mental or physical handicap.

Break (or interval) pay is no longer payable under DEA except during periods your school is closed because of an executive order of the president or an emergency (such as a natural disaster or strike). For example, if your fall term ends on December 15 and your spring term begins January 10, your January housing allowance will cover 15 days in December, and your February housing allowance will cover 21 days in January.

Scholarship and Grant Programs for Veterans

Now that your dependents have found programs to benefit them in their quest for education, it is your turn. You have a wealth of opportunities available to you. All you have to do is find them. Here are some examples of programs specifically for veterans.

Severely injured service member and spouse scholarship opportunities

In response to the severely injured service members and their spouses expressing an interest in pursuing diploma and certification programs or college degrees that will help prepare them for jobs and careers, the DOD created the Defense Activity for Non-Traditional Education Support (DANTES). The DANTES mission is to support the off-duty, voluntary education programs of the DOD and to conduct special projects and development activities in support of education-related functions of the department. This program links the members and spouses to schools that are willing and currently offer educational programs and scholarships. In addition to resources, including distance learning help, higher education information, counselor support, and education outreach, the DANTES website hosts a "scholarship search" page, located at **www.dantes.doded. mil/Sub%20Pages/Counselor_Support/Online_Scholarships.html**.

Iraqi/Afghanistan War Veterans Scholarship Fund

The AFCEA Northern Virginia (NOVA) Chapter has contributed $100,000 to establish the Iraqi/Afghanistan War Veterans Scholarship Fund. Scholarships of $2,500 each are offered to active-duty and honorably discharged U.S. military veterans (including reservists and National Guard personnel) of the Enduring Freedom (Afghanistan) or Iraqi Freedom operations who are actively pursuing an undergraduate degree in an eligible major at accredited two- or four-year institutions in the United States. Distance-learning or online programs affiliated with a major U.S. institution are eligible.

Applicants must be enrolled currently and attending either a two-year or four-year accredited college or university in the United States. Applications will be accepted from qualified freshmen, sophomore, junior, and senior undergraduate students enrolled at the time of application either part time or full time in an eligible degree program.

Candidates must be majoring in the following or C4I-related fields of electrical, aerospace, systems or computer engineering; computer engineering technology; computer network systems; information systems security; computer information systems; information systems management; technology management; electronics engineering technology; computer science; physics; mathematics; or science or mathematics education. Majors directly related to the support of U.S. intelligence or national security enterprises with relevance to the mission of AFCEA also will be eligible.

For more information about this cosponsored scholarship, visit **www.af-cea.org/education/scholarships** or **www.afceanova.org**.

Veterans' Employment and Training state grants

The Veterans' Employment and Training Service (VETS) offers employment and training services to eligible veterans through a noncompetitive Jobs for Veterans State Grants program. Under this grant program, funds are allocated to State Workforce Agencies in direct proportion to the number of veterans seeking employment within their state.

This grant provides funds to serve veterans exclusively, other eligible persons, transitioning service members, their spouses and, indirectly, employers. The grant also gives the state the flexibility to determine the most effective and efficient distribution of their staff resources.

Disabled Veterans' Outreach Program specialists

Disabled Veterans Outreach Program (DVOP) specialists provide intensive services to meet the employment needs of disabled veterans and other eligible veterans, with the maximum emphasis directed toward serving those who are economically or educationally disadvantaged, including homeless veterans, and veterans with barriers to employment. DVOP specialists are involved actively in outreach efforts to increase program participation among those with the greatest barriers to employment, which may include but should not be limited to: outplacement in Department of Veterans' Affairs (DVA) Vocational Rehabilitation and Employment Program offices; DVA Medical Centers; routine site visits to Veterans' Service Organization meetings; Native American Trust Territories; Military installations; and, other areas of known concentrations of veterans or transitioning service members. The case management approach, taught by the National Veterans' Training Institute, is generally accepted as the method to use when providing vocational guidance or related services to eligible veterans identified as needing intensive services.

Local veterans' employment representatives

Local veterans' employment representatives conduct outreach to employers and engage in advocacy efforts with hiring executives to increase employment opportunities for veterans, encourage the hiring of disabled veterans, and generally assist veterans to gain and retain employment. LVER staff conduct seminars for employers and job search workshops for veterans seeking employment and facilitate priority of service in regard to employment, training, and placement services furnished to veterans by all staff of the employment service delivery system.

To meet the specific needs of veterans, particularly veterans with barriers to employment, DVOP and LVER staff are thoroughly familiar with the full range of job development services and training programs available at the State Workforce Agency One-Stop Career Centers and Department of Veterans' Affairs Vocational Rehabilitation and Employment Program locations.

Applications for funds under the Jobs for Veterans State Grants Program will be accepted only from the designated administrative entity that operates the employment service delivery system within the state.

More Scholarships for Military Members and Dependents

Military.com provides valuable scholarships and grant information for the military community. This Internet site features a search browser (type of financial aid desired, service affiliation, educational goal), and the search results identify available internships, grants, loans, scholarships, etc. For example:

The 25th Infantry Division Association Educational Memorial Scholarship Award provides financial assistance for college to the children of veterans and current members of the 25th Infantry Division Association. Award amounts up to $1,500 are available. More information can be found at **www.25thida.com/associat.html#scholarships**.

Other sources of financial aid include the student's state government and educational institution. Often, the best source of information and assistance will be the school's financial aid office. Information about financial aid specific to individual states also may be obtained from state grant and guaranty agencies.

Chapter 11

Educational Benefits and Training Programs

ow that you know what types of scholarships you are eligible for as a veteran, what educational program should you dedicate yourself to? The VA provides a number of programs, trainings, and assistance to help you better yourself and your situation. It also includes some programs to help your spouses and dependents save money on education and training programs. Why not take advantage of some of the benefits listed throughout this chapter? This list is by no means exclusive, but it will give you a heads up as to what is out there for educating and empowering veterans in their day-to-day lives. *Chapter 12 will cover the now-famous Post-9/11 GI Bill that has radically changed educational benefits for veterans.*

Montgomery GI Bill

You already could have the means to help yourself pay for some additional education once you are done with your active duty. With the Montgomery

GI Bill (MGIB), Active Duty members enroll and pay $100 per month for 12 months and then are entitled to receive a monthly education benefit once they have completed a minimum service obligation.

The Montgomery GI Bill provides up to 36 months of education benefits to eligible veterans for:

- College, business, technical, or vocational school
- Tuition assistance
- On-the-job training and apprenticeship programs
- Correspondence courses
- Remedial, deficiency, and refresher training
- Flight training
- The cost of tests for licenses or certifications needed to get, keep, or advance in a job
- National tests

Generally, benefits are payable for ten years following your release from active duty. You may be an eligible veteran if you:

- Entered active duty for the first time after June 30, 1985

- Received a high-school diploma or equivalent (or, in some cases, 12 hours of college credit) before the end of your first obligated period of service
- Received an honorable discharge
- Continuously served for three years, two years if that is what you first enlisted for, or two years if you have an obligation to serve four years in the Selected Reserve AND entered Selected Reserve within a year of leaving active duty.

$600 buy-up program

For an additional $600 contribution, you may receive up to $5,400 in additional GI Bill benefits. The increased benefit is only payable after leaving active duty, and the additional contribution must be made while on active duty.

You may be an eligible veteran if you fit the eligibility for the MGIB benefits and you meet the requirements of one of the categories below:

CATEGORY I
- Entered active duty for the first time after June 30, 1985
- Had military pay reduced by $100 a month for first 12 months

CATEGORY II
- Entered active duty before January 1, 1977
- Served at least 1 day between October 19, 1984, and June 30, 1985, and stayed on active duty through June 30,1988 (or June 30, 1987, if you entered the Selected Reserve within one year of leaving active duty and served four years)
- On December 31, 1989, you had entitlement left from Vietnam-era GI Bill

CATEGORY III
- Not eligible for MGIB under Category I or II
- On active duty on September 30, 1990, AND separated involuntarily after February 2, 1991, involuntarily separated on or

after November 30, 1993, or voluntarily separated under either the Voluntary Separation Incentive (VSI) or Special Separation Benefit (SSB) program

- Before separation, you had military pay reduced by $1,200

CATEGORY IV

- On active duty on October 9, 1996, AND you had money remaining in a VEAP account on that date and you elected MGIB by October 9, 1997, or entered full-time National Guard duty under title 32, USC, between July 1, 1985, and November 28, 1989, and you elected MGIB during the period October 9, 1996, through July 8, 1997

- Had military pay reduced by $100 a month for 12 months or made a $1,200 lump-sum contribution

The monthly benefit paid to you is based on the type of training you take, length of your service, your category, and if DOD put extra money in your MGIB Fund (called "kickers"). You can apply by filling out VA Form 22-1990, Application for Education Benefits.

Montgomery GI Bill — Selected Reserve

The MGIB-SR program may be available to you if you are a member of the Selected Reserve. The Selected Reserve includes the Army Reserve, Navy Reserve, Air Force Reserve, Marine Corps Reserve and Coast Guard Reserve, and the Army National Guard and the Air National Guard. Your eligibility for the program normally ends on the day you leave the Selected Reserve.

One exception to this rule exists if you are mobilized (or recalled to active duty from your reserve status), in this case your eligibility may be extended for the time you are mobilized PLUS four months. For example, if you are mobilized for 12 months, your eligibility period is extended for 16 months (12 months active duty PLUS 4 months.)

To qualify, you must meet the following requirements:

- Have a six-year obligation to serve in the Selected Reserve signed after June 30, 1985. If you are an officer, you must have agreed to serve six years in addition to your original obligation. For some types of training, it is necessary to have a six-year commitment that begins after September 30, 1990.

- Complete your initial active duty for training (IADT)

- Receive a high school diploma or equivalency certificate before completing IADT. You may not use 12 hours toward a college degree to meet this requirement.

- Remain in good standing while serving in an active Selected Reserve unit. You will also retain MGIB - SR eligibility if you were discharged from Selected Reserve service due to a disability that was not caused by misconduct. Your eligibility period may be extended if you are ordered to active duty.

Your unit will give you a DD Form 2384-1, Notice of Basic Eligibility, when you become eligible for the program. Your unit also will code your eligibility into the Department of Defense personnel system so that VA may verify your eligibility. Make sure your selected program is approved for VA training. If you are not clear on this point, VA will inform you and the school or company about the requirements.

Obtain and complete VA Form 22-1990, Application for Education Benefits. Send it to the VA regional office with jurisdiction over the state where you will train. If you have started training, take your application and your Notice of Basic Eligibility to your school or employer. Ask them to complete VA Form 22-1999, (not available online) Enrollment Certification, and send all the forms to VA.

Post-Vietnam Veterans' Educational Assistance Program (VEAP)

The Post-Vietnam Veterans' Educational Assistance Program (VEAP) is an education benefit for veterans who paid into VEAP while they were in the service. Eligible veterans may be entitled to as much as 36 months of training. Eligibility usually ends ten years after getting out of the service, but the time limit can be longer in certain cases. Eligible veterans may pursue any of the following types of training:

- College or university programs
- Correspondence courses
- Business, technical or vocational training
- Flight training
- On-the-job training and apprenticeship programs
- High school diploma or equivalent
- Remedial, deficiency, and refresher training
- The cost of tests for licenses or certifications needed to get, keep, or advance a job
- National tests

To establish eligibility for VEAP, you must have

- First entered active duty after December 31, 1976, and before July 1, 1985
- Contributed to VEAP before April 1, 1987
- Completed your first period of service
- Been discharged under conditions other than dishonorable

The total dollar amount of your benefits is the sum of your total contributions plus matching funds from VA equal to two times your contributions plus any DOD contributions.

The monthly amount you will receive is based on the total from above, the number of months you contributed, the type of training you are pursuing, and your training time (i.e. full-time, half-time). Contributions may be refunded.

When you find a program approved for VA training, you can apply for VEAP by completing VA Form 22-1990, Application for Education Benefits. You also can apply online at **http://vabenefits.vba.va.gov/vonapp**.

National Testing Programs (CLEP, DSST, Excelsior)

DANTES and CLEP tests are a fast track to a college degree. *DANTAS was first introduced in the last chapter; refer back to it for more information.* As a veteran, you are entitled to participate in National Testing Program. Currently, the approved tests are:

- SAT (Scholastic Assessment Test)
- LSAT (Law School Admission Test)
- GRE (Graduate Record Exam)
- GMAT (Graduate Management Admission Test)
- AP (Advanced Placement Exam)
- CLEP (College-Level Examination Program)
- ACT (American College Testing Program)
- DAT (Dental Admissions Test)
- MAT (Miller Analogies Test)
- MCAT (Medical College Admissions Test)
- OAT (Optometry Admissions Testing)
- PCAT (Pharmacy College Admissions Test)
- TOEFL (Test of English as a Foreign Language)
- DSST (DANTES Subject Standardized Tests)
- ECE (Excelsior College Examinations)

The VA will reimburse a person for required test fees. However, the VA has no authority to reimburse a person for any optional costs related to the testing process.

Test fees that VA will reimburse include:

- Registration fees
- Fees for specialized tests
- Administrative fees

Fees VA will not reimburse include:

- Fees to take pretests (such as Kaplan tests)

- Fees to receive scores quickly
- Other costs or fees for optional items that are not required to take an approved test

Every applicant for reimbursement for a national test must have filed an original application and have been found eligible. The best way to claim the benefit is to submit the following:

- A copy of your test results
- A signed note or a signed VA Form 21-4138, Statement in Support of Claim, stating that you are requesting reimbursement for the cost of a national test.

The following information is required:

- Name of the test
- Name of the organization offering the test
- Date the person took the test
- Cost of taking the test

General Rule Regarding Receipts: You normally do not have to submit a receipt or proof of payment for the cost. However, in certain instances, it is necessary to submit this evidence. These situations are the following

- DSST Tests (DANTES Subject Standardized Tests)
- Certain situations regarding the CLEP, MAT, and PCAT tests

DANTES, CLEP, and Excelsior tests are accepted at most universities and colleges and can earn you three to six semester hours (upper and lower level) college credit by exam. DANTES has vast amounts of information, study guides, course information, and more on their website. It is one of the most valuable resources you will find to further your education. The DANTES website is **www.dantes.doded.mil/Dantes_web/DANTESHOME.asp**.

Troops to Teachers

If you want to use your considerable skills learned in the military to educate others, Troops to Teachers provides referral assistance and placement services to military personnel interested in beginning a second career in public education as a teacher. The DANTES Troops to Teachers office will help applicants identify teacher certification requirements, programs leading to certification, and employment opportunities.

The primary objective of TTT is to help recruit quality teachers for schools that serve students from low-income families throughout America. TTT helps relieve teacher shortages, especially in math, science, special education, and other critical subject areas and assists military personnel in making successful transitions to second careers in teaching.

Funding has been appropriated to provide financial assistance to eligible participants, provide placement assistance, referral services, and maintain a network of state offices. Military personnel interested in a second career in public education may submit a registration form to DANTES.

A network of state TTT offices has been established to provide participants with counseling and assistance regarding certification requirements, routes to state certification, and employment leads. The TTT homepage provides information and resource links, including a job referral system to allow participants to search for job vacancies and links to state Departments of Education, state certification offices, model resumes, and other job listing sites in public education.

Pending availability of funds, financial assistance may be provided to eligible individuals as stipends up to $5K to help pay for teacher certification costs or as bonuses of $10K to teach in schools serving a high percentage of students from low-income families. Participants who accept the stipend or bonus must agree to teach for three years in targeted schools in accordance with the authorizing legislation.

Register with Troops to Teachers by downloading a registration form from **www.ProudToServeAgain.com**. Eligible active duty and reserve personnel may register with Troops to Teachers at any time. Counseling and information are available to all participants; however, financial assistance may not be provided to active duty personnel until one year before retirement.

Reserve Educational Assistance (REAP)

REAP is a DOD education benefit program designed to provide educational assistance to members of the Reserve components called or ordered to active duty in response to a war or national emergency (contingency operation) as declared by the president or Congress. This program makes certain reservists who were activated for at least 90 days after September 11, 2001, either eligible for education benefits or eligible for increased benefits.

The REAP program offers the same buy-up program offered by the MGIB program seen earlier in this chapter. Therefore, some reservists may contribute up to an additional $600 to the GI Bill to receive increased monthly benefits. For an additional $600 contribution, you may receive up to $5,400 in additional GI Bill benefits. You must be a member of a Ready Reserve component (Selected Reserve, Individual Ready Reserve, or Inactive National Guard) to pay into the "buy-up" program. Refer back to the qualifications earlier in this chapter to see if you are eligible.

Department of Labor Benefits

The Department of Labor's Employment and Training Administration offers a host of services to military spouses through its extensive network of One-Stop Career Centers and the CareerOneStop Electronic Tools that are broadly available to the general population.

One-Stop Career Centers are the focal point of the workforce investment system, supporting the employment needs of job seekers and the human resource needs of business. The range of services for job seekers includes skill and need assessments, job counseling, local labor market information on high-growth occupations, job training/retraining and placement, and other services provided through strategic partnerships with organizations in their community.

In addition, a number of military spouses (including surviving spouses) receive services through discretionary National Emergency Grants should states choose to apply. These grants provide employment-related assistance to members of the National Guard and Military Reserve who were required to interrupt or postpone these services in order to fulfill deployment requirements in active duty.

The major areas covered include the following:

- Expanded employment and training services for military spouses through DOD Family Centers and DOL One-Stop Career Centers
- Connections to DOL's National Business Partners
- Spouse Telework Employment Program (STEP)
- Expanded employment and training services
- Expanded training opportunities: The Labor Department has explored opportunities for expanding military spouse participation in existing employment and training programs, such as apprenticeship and the Workforce Investment Act (WIA) Dislocated Worker program.
- Connections to DOL's national business partners: The Departments of Labor (DOL) and Defense (DOD) expanded electronic links

with DOL's national business partners to promote the hiring of military spouses and transitioning military personnel. DOL has been actively connecting spouses with DOL national business partners by sending information to all business partners about military spouses.

More information may be found at the military spouse website, **www.mil-spouse.org**.

National Call To Service Program

This National Call to Service Incentive program requires a participant to perform a period of national service to be eligible for benefits. There is a three-tiered service requirement to qualify for incentives under the National Call to Service program:

First, after completion of initial entry training, individuals must serve on active duty in a military occupational specialty designated by the secretary of defense for a period of 15 months. After this, and without a break in service, these individuals must serve either an additional period of active duty as determined by the secretary of defense or a period of 24 months in an active status in the Selected Reserve. After completion of this period of service, the remaining period of obligated service specified in the agreement will be served as follows:

- On active duty in the armed forces
- In the Selected Reserve
- In the Individual Ready Reserve
- In Americorps, or another domestic national service program jointly designated by the secretary of defense and the head of such a program
- Any combination of the service referred to above also may be approved by the secretary of the military department concerned pursuant to regulations prescribed by the secretary of defense and specified in the agreement.

Choice of incentives

Individuals who participate in this new program have a choice of incentives as follows:

- Cash bonus of $5,000
- Repayment of a qualifying student loan not to exceed $18,000
- Entitlement to allowance equal to the three-year monthly Chapter 30 rate for 12 months
- Entitlement to allowance equal to 50 percent of the less than three-year monthly Chapter 30 rate for 36 months
- Coordination with Montgomery GI Bill benefits. *These benefits were discussed earlier in the chapter.*

Chapter 12

The Post-9/11 GI Bill

The Post-9/11 GI Bill is the most impressive educational benefit package to be announced in recent years. It was signed into law as of July 2008. The bill went into effect August 1, 2009. In summary, the Post-9/11 GI Bill provides financial support for education and housing to individuals

with at least 90 days of aggregate service. It is a 36-month benefit designed to cover four years of college, minus summers or four nine-month semesters of college.

Approved training under the Post-9/11 GI Bill includes graduate and undergraduate degrees, vocational/technical training, on-the-job training, flight training, correspondence training, licensing and national testing programs, and tutorial assistance. All training programs must be approved for GI Bill benefits.

The benefit packages are designed based on the number of active days of service. This gives non-active, as well as previously active, service members the chance at the same benefits as active service members. However the benefit is prorated for 36 months, and at 36 months of service, you earn full benefits. Generally, benefits are payable for 15 years following your release from active duty.

As you will read in this chapter, there have been several sweeping changes to the Post-9/11 GI Bill. You have to be thorough in your research to understand clearly your benefits. This chapter will give you a broad over-view as well as provide you resources to search for more information. This website has the latest information about this program: **www.gibill.va.gov**.

A Note from the Author

I have used the Post-9/11 GI Bill for the past three years. I transferred 27 months of benefits to my son Jordan, who is in his final year of law school at the University of Texas. Because of this amazing program, he will graduate law school debt free. I transferred the remaining nine months of benefits to my youngest son, Colton, who used it for his first year of college at the University of Florida. The Post-9/11 GI Bill saved more than $160,000 for Jordan's law school tuition and housing costs (at the in-state tuition rate) and more than $20,000 in tuition and housing costs for Colton's first year. And this program cost me nothing.

Under the new bill, there are benefits for members attending certified colleges and universities. Some members may be eligible for educational or skills training programs. However, the bill does not cover educational expenses incurred before July 31, 2009.

Under the Post-9/11 GI Bill, up to 100 percent of college tuition and fees may be covered. There are stipulations for eligibility and the type of school expenses. If found eligible, the payment goes directly to the school to cover the costs of tuition and any other fees related to school expenses. This payment may not exceed the highest undergraduate fees of an institution of higher learning. The rate used to calculate these fees will be based on the state where the school is located, not where the student lives. The benefit amount the student will receive is based on where he or she lives, where the school is located, and what type of degree or certificate the student is pursuing.

Other benefits for active or reserve service members are the monthly housing allowance and a book and supplies allowance. *More details about these will be provided later in the chapter.* To apply, complete and submit the application form available online at **www.gibill.va.gov/apply-for-benefits**.

Eligibility

The Post-9/11 GI Bill provides support to individuals with at least 90 days of aggregate service on or after September 11, 2001, or individuals discharged with a service-connected disability after 30 days. You must have received an honorable discharge eligible for the Post-9/11 GI Bill. There are stipulations as to who is eligible to apply and what benefits are available.

All benefit amounts are based on the number of credited, active years of service an individual has as of September 10, 2001. The following table applies to all qualified service members:

Post-9/11 Service	Percentage of Maximum Amount Payable
At least 36 cumulative months (Includes entry level or skills training time)	100%
At least 30 continuous days on active duty and discharged due to service-connected disability (Includes entry level or skills training time)	100%
At least 30 cumulative months (Includes entry level or skills training time)	90%
At least 24 cumulative months (Cannot include entry level or skills training time)	80%
At least 18 cumulative months (Cannot include entry level or skills training time))	70%

Post-9/11 Service	Percentage of Maximum Amount Payable
At least 12 cumulative months (Cannot include entry level or skills training time)	60%
At least six cumulative months (Cannot include entry level or skills training time)	50%
90 aggregate days (Cannot include entry level or skills training time)	40%

You must have 90 days of active duty service after September 10, 2001, and:

- Be honorably discharged from the military
- Be released from service honorably and placed on the retired list, temporarily disabled retired list or transferred to either the Fleet Reserve or the Fleet Marine Corps Reserve
- Be released from service with characterization of honorable to complete further service as a reservist
- Be released from service for any of the following reasons: EPTS (existed prior to service), HDSP (hardship), CIWD (condition interfered with duty)

Coverage

The Post 9-11 GI Bill will pay eligible individuals:

- Full tuition and fees directly to the school for all public school in-state students. For those attending private or foreign schools, tuition and fees are capped at $17,500 per academic year. If you are attending a private institution of higher learning in Arizona, Michigan, New Hampshire, New York, Pennsylvania, South Carolina, or Texas, you may be eligible for a higher tuition reimbursement rate.

- For those attending a more expensive private school or a public school as a nonresident out-of-state student, a program exists that may help to reimburse the difference. This program is called the "Yellow Ribbon Program," which will be covered in the next section.

- A monthly housing allowance (MHA) based on the Basic Allowance for Housing for an E-5 with dependents at the location of the school. For those enrolled solely in distance learning, the housing allowance payable is equal to half the national average BAH for an E-5 with dependents ($673.50 for the 2011 academic year). For those attending foreign schools (schools without a main campus in the U.S.) the BAH rate is fixed at $1,347.00 for the 2011 academic year. Active duty students and their spouses cannot receive the MHA.

- An annual books and supplies stipend of $1,000 paid proportionately based on enrollment. This stipend is paid to the school at the beginning of each term. The number of credit hours taken by the student (not to exceed $41 per credit hour) determines the amount of the stipend.

- A one time payment of $500 may be payable to certain individuals relocating from highly rural areas.

Restoring GI Bill Fairness Act of 2011

On August 3, 2011, President Obama signed the Restoring GI Bill Fairness Act of 2011 into law, amending the Post-9/11 GI Bill. The new legislation authorizes VA to pay more than $17,500 (or the appropriately reduced amount based on your eligibility percentage) in tuition and fees under the Post-9/11 GI Bill for certain students attending private colleges and universities in seven states: Arizona, Michigan, New Hampshire, New York, Pennsylvania, South Carolina, and Texas.

To qualify for the increased payment (also referred to as the "grandfathered" tuition and fee amount), students must have been enrolled in the same college or university since January 4, 2011, and must have been enrolled in a program for which the combined amount of tuition and fees for full-time attendance during the 2010-2011 academic year exceeded $17,500.

If you meet the requirements and your tuition and fee charges for the academic year exceed $17,500, VA will pay you a percentage (based on your eligibility tier) of the greater of $17,500, or the amount you would have been paid for your training during the 2010-2011 academic year (based on the tuition and fee in-state maximums). The 2010 to 2011 in-state maximums are listed at **http:// gibill.va.gov/gi_bill_info/ch33/tuition_and_fees_2010.htm**.

You will receive the "grandfathered" rate for tuition and fees for all terms that begin before August 1, 2014, as long as you are continuously enrolled at the same institution. If you transfer to a different institution, even if it is located in the same state, you will no longer qualify for the "grandfathered" rate.

The Yellow Ribbon Program

Institutions of higher learning (degree granting institutions) may elect to participate in the Yellow Ribbon Program to make additional funds available for your education program without an additional charge to your GI Bill entitlement. Institutions that voluntarily enter into a Yellow Ribbon Agreement with VA choose the amount of tuition and fees that will be contributed. VA will match that amount and issue payment directly to the institution. You must be enrolled in an approved program offered by an IHL. You can search for schools that participate in the Yellow Ribbon program at **www.gi-bill.va.gov/gi_bill_info/ch33/yrp/ yrp_list_2011.htm**.

Under the Yellow Ribbon Program, the Post-9/11 GI Bill will pay you:

- All resident tuition and fees for a public school
- The higher of the actual tuition and fees or $17,500 per academic year for a private school. Your actual tuition and fees costs may exceed these amounts if you are attending a private school or are attending a public school as a nonresident student.

Schools that intend to participate in the Yellow Ribbon Program will establish application procedures for eligible students. The school will determine the maximum number of students that may participate in the program and the percent of tuition that will be contributed.

If your school has volunteered to participate in the Yellow Ribbon Program, you should take your Certificate of Eligibility to your school and ask your school to certify your enrollment to VA, including Yellow Ribbon. You cannot certify your participation in the Yellow Ribbon Program directly to the VA. Your school must report this information on your enrollment certification.

Post-9/11 GI Bill Transferability

For the first time in history, service members enrolled in the Post-9/11 GI Bill program will be able to transfer unused educational benefits to their spouses or children. There are stipulations to this provision and eligibility requirements to determine immediate family members. Individuals eligible to transfer their benefits include all members of the military; this includes enlisted members, active reserves, and officers. Service must have started on or before August 1, 2009.

An eligible service member may transfer up to the total months of unused Post-9/11 GI Bill benefits or the entire 36 months if the member has used none (unless DOD/DHS limits the number of months an individual may transfer).

The service member must have six years of service on or before the date of transfer and must agree to serve four more years after the date of transfer or have at least ten years of service on or before the date of transfer. In this case, the additional four years is waived as long as the service member agrees to complete his or her current term.

The service member must become eligible for retirement from the military during the period of August 1, 2009, through August 1, 2013. A service member is considered to be eligible for retirement after completing 20 years of active service or 20 qualifying years of reserve service. Service members eligible to retire on August 1, 2009, would not have to fulfill any further terms of service. Individuals with a retirement date after August 1, 2009, and before July 1, 2010, would not be required to complete any further service. Individuals eligible to retire after August 1, 2009, but before August 1, 2010, would need to agree to one more year of service after the transfer has been approved.

Ground Zero Memorial, New York City

Service members eligible for retirement on or after August 1, 2010, and before August 1, 2011, would need to serve two more years of service after the transfer has been approved. Individuals eligible for retirement on or after August 1, 2011, but before August 1, 2012, would have to agree to serve three more years after the transfer has been approved.

Eligible dependents

An individual approved to transfer an entitlement to educational assistance under this section may transfer the individual's entitlement to:

- The individual's spouse
- One or more of the individual's children
- Any combination of spouse and child

A family member must be enrolled in the Defense Eligibility Enrollment Reporting System (DEERS) and be eligible for benefits at the time of transfer. A child's subsequent marriage will not affect his or her eligibility to receive the educational benefit; however, after an individual has designated a child as a transferee under this section, the individual retains the right to revoke or modify the transfer at any time.

Family member use of transferred educational benefits is subject to the following:

Spouse:

- May start to use the benefit immediately
- May use the benefit while the member remains in the Armed Forces or after separation from active duty
- Is not eligible for the monthly stipend or books and supplies stipend while the member is serving on active duty
- Can use the benefit for up to 15 years after the service member's last separation from active duty

Child:

- May start to use the benefit only after the individual making the transfer has completed at least ten years of service in the Armed Forces
- May use the benefit while the eligible individual remains in the Armed Forces or after separation from active duty
- May not use the benefit until he/she has attained a secondary school diploma (or equivalency certificate) or reached age 18

- Is entitled to the monthly stipend and books and supplies stipend even though the eligible individual is on active duty
- Is not subject to the 15-year delimiting date but may not use the benefit after reaching 26 years of age

You can initiate your transfer at **www.defense.gov/home/features/2009 /0409_gibill**. Upon approval, family members may apply to use transferred benefits with VA by completing VA Form 22-1990e. VA Form 22-1990e should only be completed and submitted to VA by the family member after DOD has approved the request. Do not use VA Form 22-1990e to apply.

Marine Gunnery Sergeant John David Fry Scholarship

The Marine Gunnery Sergeant John David Fry Scholarship amends the Post-9/11 GI Bill to include the children of service members who die in the line of duty after Sept. 10, 2001. Eligible children attending school may receive the same benefits a veteran participating in the Post-9/11 GI Bill.

Children of an active duty member of the Armed Forces who has died in the line of duty on or after September 11, 2001, are eligible for this benefit. A child may be married or over 23 and still be eligible.

Eligible children:

- Are entitled to 36 months of benefits at the 100 percent level
- Have 15 years to use the benefit beginning on his/her 18th birthday
- May use the benefit until his or her 33rd birthday
- Cannot use benefit before age 18, even if he or she has completed high school
- Are not eligible for the Yellow Ribbon Program

A new version of the VA Form 22-5490, "Dependents' Application for VA Education Benefits" is available by going to VA's website, **www.gibill. va.gov**, and clicking on "Apply for Benefits." Paper versions of the form also may be printed. A parent or guardian must sign the application if the child is under age 18.

The Post-9/11 GI Bill compared to other benefits

Some dependents might qualify for more than one set of benefits according to their parents' or their own eligibility. You may receive a maximum of 48 months of benefits combined if you are eligible for more than one VA education program. Spouses generally are eligible to receive benefits for ten years. However, spouses of individuals rated totally and permanently disabled within three years of discharge and spouses of individuals who die on active duty are granted a 20-year eligibility period. The VA can pay the difference between the total cost of tuition and fees and the amount of tuition assistance paid by the military.

The following chart illustrates the benefits of the Post-9/11 GI Bill compared to some of the other educational assistance programs:

	Post-9/11 GI Bill	MGIB-AD	MGIB-SR	REAP	VEAP	DEA
Minimum Length of Service	90 days active aggregate service (after 9/10/01) or 30 days continuous if discharged for disability	2 yr. continuous enlistment (minimum duty varies by service date, branch, etc.)	6 yr. commitment (after 6/30/85)	90 days active continuous service (after 9/10/01)	181 continuous days active service (between 12/31/76 and 7/1/85)	Not applicable
Maximum # of Months of Benefits	36	36	36	36	36	45

	Post-9/11 GI Bill	MGIB-AD	MGIB-SR	REAP	VEAP	DEA
How Payments Are Made	Tuition: paid to school Housing stipend: paid monthly to student Books & supplies: paid to student at the beginning of the term	Paid to student	Paid to student	Paid to student	Paid to student	Paid to student
Duration of Benefits	Generally 15 years from last day of active duty	Generally 10 years from last day of active duty	Ends the day you leave Selected Reserve	Generally 10 years from the day you leave the Selected Reserve or the day you leave the IRR	10 yrs. from last day of active duty	Spouse: 10 - 20 years Child: Ages 18-26
Degree Training	Yes	Yes	Yes	Yes	Yes	Yes
Non College Degree Training	Yes	Yes	Yes	Yes	Yes	Yes
On-the-Job & Apprenticeship Training	Yes	Yes	Yes	Yes	Yes	Yes
Flight Training	Yes	Yes	Yes	Yes	Yes	Yes
Correspondence Courses	Yes	Yes	Yes	Yes	Yes	Yes
Licensing & Certification	Yes	Yes	Yes	Yes	Yes	Yes
National Testing Programs	Yes	Yes	Yes	Yes	Yes	Yes
Work-Study Program	Yes	Yes	Yes	Yes	Yes	Yes
Tutorial Assistance [5]	Yes	Yes	Yes	No	Yes	Yes

Chapter 13

Assistance for Homeless Veterans

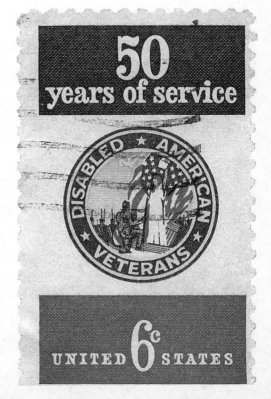

t is staggering how many of our homeless citizens are also military veterans of the armed forces. One-third of adult homeless men and nearly one-quarter of all homeless adults have served in the armed forces. Although there is no true measure of the number of homeless veterans, it has been estimated that almost 200,000 veterans may be homeless on any given night and that twice as many veterans experience homelessness during a year. Many other veterans are considered at risk because of poverty, lack of support from family and friends, and precarious living conditions in overcrowded or substandard housing. Ninety-seven percent of homeless veterans are male, and the vast majority are single. About half of all homeless veterans suffer from mental illness and more than two-thirds suffer from alcohol or drug abuse problems. Nearly 40 percent have both psychiatric and substance abuse disorders. Many of these individuals suffer mental and physical ailments caused by their military service. Most do not realize specific programs are in place to assist them.

Last year, the VA provided health care services to more than 100,000 homeless veterans and provided services to 70,000 veterans in its specialized homeless programs. More than 40,000 homeless veterans receive compensation or pension benefits annually. Although limited to veterans and their dependents, VA's major homeless programs offer a wide array of services and initiatives to help veterans recover from homelessness and live as self-sufficiently and independently as possible.

Direct Benefit Programs for Veterans

The term "homeless" or "homeless individual" or "homeless person" includes:

- An individual who lacks a fixed, regular, and adequate nighttime residence

- An individual who has a primary nighttime residence that is a supervised publicly or privately operated shelter designed to provide temporary living accommodations (including welfare hotels, congregate shelters, and transitional housing for the mentally ill); an institution that provides a temporary residence for individuals intended to be institutionalized; or a public or private place not designed for, or ordinarily used as, a regular sleeping accommodation for human beings"

The VA has many programs that directly benefit homeless veterans. These programs range from the basics, providing shelter and food, to long-term solution programs offering rehabilitation training and health care.

Homeless coordinators at VA regional offices provide outreach services and help expedite the processing of homeless veterans' claims. The Homeless Eligibility Clarification Act allows eligible veterans without a fixed address to receive VA benefits checks at VA regional offices. VA also has procedures to expedite the processing of homeless veterans' benefits claims. Last year more than 35,000 homeless veterans received assistance and nearly 4,000 had their claims expedited by Veterans Benefits Administration staff members.

VA's Health Care for Homeless Veterans Program (HCHV) operates at 133 sites, where extensive outreach, physical and psychiatric health exams, treatment, referrals and ongoing case management are provided to homeless veterans with mental health problems, including substance abuse.

Work-Therapy (CWT) and Compensated Work-Therapy/Transitional Residence (TR) programs

Through its Veterans Industry/Compensated Work-Therapy (CWT) and Compensated Work-Therapy/Transitional Residence (TR) programs, VA offers structured work opportunities and supervised therapeutic housing for at-risk and homeless veterans with physical, psychiatric, and substance abuse disorders. VA contracts with private industry and the public sector for work by these veterans, who learn new job skills, re-learn successful work habits, and regain a sense of self-esteem and self-worth. Veterans are paid for their work and, in turn, make a payment toward maintenance and upkeep of the residence. Details about this program are available at **www. cwt.va.gov/index.asp**.

Veterans in the CWT/TR program work about 33 hours per week with approximate earnings of $732 per month and pay an average of $186 per month toward maintenance and up-keep of the residence. The average length of stay is about 174 days.

VA operates 66 homes with more than 520 beds in transitional residences. Nine sites with 18 houses serve homeless veterans exclusively and two-thirds of all CWT and TR beds serve homeless veterans. There are more than 110 CWT operations nationwide.

Using a business model, VI/CWT program staff specializes in working with facility management, human resource, and/or production personnel to address labor force deficits. Over the years VI/CWT veterans have been employed successfully in various competitive positions including health care, information technology, manufacturing, warehousing, construction trades, clerical and office support, retail, and the services delivery.

About 14,000 veterans participate in CWT programs annually. VA's National Cemetery Administration and Veterans Health Administration have formed partnerships at national cemeteries, where formerly homeless veterans from the CWT program have received therapeutic work opportunities while providing VA cemeteries with a supplemental work force.

For more information, contact:

Employer Services: Charles McGeough in Dallas, Texas, at Charles. McGeough@va.gov

Veteran Services: Donna Tasker in Biloxi, Mississippi, at Donna. Tasker@va.gov

Transitional Residence: Jamie Ploppert in Hampton, Virginia, at Jamie. Ploppert2@va.gov

Stand Downs

The original Stand Down for homeless veterans was modeled after the Stand Down concept used during the Vietnam War to provide a safe retreat for units returning from combat operations. At secure base camp areas, troops were able to take care of personal hygiene, get clean uniforms, enjoy warm meals, receive medical and dental care, mail and receive letters, and enjoy the camaraderie of friends in a safe environment. Stand Down afforded battle-weary soldiers the opportunity to renew their spirit, health, and overall sense of well-being.

That is the purpose of the Stand Down for homeless veterans, and achieving those objectives requires a wide range of support services and time. The program is successful because it brings these services to one location, making them more accessible to homeless veterans. Stand Downs are collaborative one- to three-day events, coordinated between local VAs, other government agencies, and community agencies that serve the homeless. In many locations, Stand Downs provide health screenings, referral and access to long-term treatment, benefits counseling, ID cards and access to other programs to meet their immediate needs. Each year, VA participates in more than 100 Stand Downs coordinated by local entities. Surveys show that more than 23,000 veterans and family members attend these events with more than 13,000 volunteers contributing annually. Ideally, Stand Downs are used to help veterans connect with long-term assistance programs available through the VA. Details may be found at **www.va.gov/ HOMELESS/StandDown.asp or www.nchv.org/standdown.cfm.**

The Domiciliary Care for Homeless Veterans (DCHV)

The Domiciliary Care Program is the Department of Veterans Affairs' (VA) oldest health care program. Established in the late 1860s, the domiciliary's original purpose was to provide a home for disabled volunteer soldiers of the Civil War. Domiciliary has evolved from a "soldiers' home" to become an active clinical rehabilitation and treatment program for male and female veterans, and domiciliary programs are is now integrated with the Mental Health Residential Rehabilitation and Treatment Programs (MH RRTPs). Details on this program may be found at **www.va.gov/homeless/dchv.asp.**

HUD-VASH

This joint Supported Housing Program with the Department of Housing and Urban Development provides permanent housing and ongoing treatment services to the harder-to-serve homeless mentally ill veterans and those suffering from substance abuse disorders. HUD's Section 8 Voucher

Program has designated 1,780 vouchers worth $44.5 million for homeless chronically mentally ill veterans. VA staff at 35 sites provide outreach, clinical care, and ongoing case management services. Rigorous evaluation of this program indicates that this approach significantly reduces days of homelessness for veterans plagued by serious mental illness and substance abuse disorders.

Veterans must be VA health care eligible veterans and must meet the definition of "homeless" found at the beginning of this chapter. Veterans must need case management services in order to obtain and sustain independent community housing. Veterans who need case management services have serious mental illness, substance use disorder history, or physical disability. Eligible candidates for the program are expected to participate in case management and use the supportive services, treatment recommendations, and assistance needed to successfully maintain recovery and sustain housing in the community.

HUD-VASH provides permanent housing for eligible homeless veterans who are single or eligible homeless veterans with families. Because HUD-VASH provides for veterans with medical, mental health, and/or substance use disorders, eligible veterans must be able to complete activities of daily living and live independently in the community with case management and supportive services.

To apply for HUD-VASH, please contact your local VA Homeless Program. Veterans can contact the HUD-VASH program directly or obtain a referral from a case manager in another VA program, from a community program, or other referral sources. Detailed information may be found at **www.va.gov/HOMELESS/docs/hud-vash_qanda_chart_10-13-09.pdf**.

Comprehensive Homeless Centers

VA's Comprehensive Homeless Centers (CHCs) place the full range of VA homeless efforts in a single medical center's catchment area and coordinate administration within a centralized framework. With extensive collaboration among non-VA service providers, VA's CHCs in Anchorage, Alaska;

Brooklyn, New York; Cleveland, Ohio; Dallas, Texas; Little Rock, Arkansas; Pittsburgh, Pennsylvania; San Francisco, California; and West Los Angles, California, provide a comprehensive continuum of care that reaches out to homeless veterans and helps them escape homelessness through a variety of treatment programs. In addition, Readjustment Counseling Service's Vet Centers provide outreach, psychological counseling, supportive social services, and referrals to other VA and community programs. Every Vet Center has a homeless veteran coordinator assigned to make sure services for homeless veterans are tailored to local needs.

The Department of Veterans Affairs' (VA) has founded a National Call Center for Homeless Veterans hotline to ensure that homeless veterans or veterans at-risk for homelessness have free, 24/7 access to trained counselors. The hotline is intended to assist homeless veterans and their families, VA Medical Centers, federal, state, and local partners, community agencies, service providers, and others in the community. To be connected with a trained VA staff member call 877-4AID VET (877-424-3838).

Excess Property for Homeless Veterans initiative

This initiative provides for the distribution of personal property, such as hats, parkas, footwear, socks, sleeping bags, and other items to homeless veterans and homeless veteran programs through VA domiciliary and other outreach activities. This initiative has been responsible for the distribution of more than $125 million in material and currently has more than $15 million in inventory. This initiative employs formerly homeless veterans to receive, house, and ship these goods to homeless programs across the country that assist veterans. Details on this program are available at **www. va.gov/HOMELESS/benefits.asp**.

Homeless Veterans Reintegration Program

The purpose of the Homeless Veterans' Reintegration Program (HVRP) is to provide services to assist in reintegrating homeless veterans into meaningful employment within the labor force and to stimulate the development of effective service delivery systems that will address the complex problems facing homeless veterans.

The Homeless Veterans Reintegration Program (HVRP) is the only federal program wholly dedicated to providing employment assistance to homeless veterans. HVRP programs fill a special need because they serve veterans who may be shunned by other programs and services because of problems such as severe post-traumatic stress disorder (PTSD), long histories of substance abuse, serious psychosocial problems, legal issues, and an HIV-positive rating. These veterans require more time-consuming, specialized, intensive assessment, referrals, and counseling than is possible in other programs that work with veterans seeking employment.

The employment focus of HVRP distinguishes it from most other programs for the homeless, which concentrate on more immediate needs such as emergency shelter, food, and substance abuse treatment. Although these are critical components of any homeless program, and grantees are required to demonstrate that their clients' needs in those areas are met, the objective of HVRP programs is to enable homeless veterans to secure and keep jobs that will allow them to re-enter mainstream society as productive citizens.

Grantees provide an array of services using a case management approach that directly assists homeless veterans as well as provides critical linkages for a variety of supportive services available in their local communities. Job placement, training, job development, career counseling, resume preparation, are among the services provided. Supportive services such as clothing, provision of or referral to temporary, transitional, and permanent housing, referral to medical and substance abuse treatment, and transportation assistance also are provided to meet the needs of this target group.

Since its inception, HVRP has featured an outreach component using veterans who themselves have experienced homelessness. In recent years, this successful technique was modified to allow the programs to use formerly homeless veterans in various other positions in which there is direct client contact such as counseling, peer coaching, intake, and follow-up services.

Contact your nearest Vet Center or call 877-4-AID-VET for more information or to apply for this program.

Homeless Providers Grant and Per Diem Program

The Homeless Providers Grant and Per Diem Program provides grants and per diem payments to help public and nonprofit organizations establish and operate new supportive housing and service centers for homeless veterans. Grant funds also may be used to purchase vans to conduct outreach or provide transportation for homeless veterans. Since the program's inception in fiscal year 1994, VA has awarded more than 400 grants to faith and community-based service providers, state or local government agencies and Native American tribal governments in 50 states and the District of Columbia. Up to 20,000 homeless veterans are provided supported housing under this program annually in the more than 10,000 beds.

Only programs with supportive housing (up to 24 months) or service centers (offering services such as case management, education, crisis intervention, counseling, etc.) are eligible for these funds. The program has two levels of funding: the Grant Component and the Per Diem Component.

Grants: Limit is 65 percent of the costs of construction, renovation, or acquisition of a building for use as service centers or transitional housing for homeless vets. Renovation of VA properties is allowed; acquiring VA properties is not. Recipients must obtain the matching 35 percent share from other sources. Grants may not be used for operational costs, including salaries.

Per Diem: Priority in awarding the Per Diem funds goes to the recipients of grants. Non-grant programs may apply for Per Diem under a separate announcement, when published in the Federal Register, announcing the funding for "Per Diem Only."

Operational costs, including salaries, may be funded by the Per Diem component. For supportive housing, the maximum amount payable under the per diem is $33.01. Veterans in supportive housing may be asked to pay rent if it does not exceed 30 percent of the veteran's monthly adjusted income. In addition, "reasonable" fees may be charged for services not paid with Per Diem funds. The maximum hourly per diem rate for a service center not connected with supportive housing is one-eighth of the daily cost of care, not to exceed the current VA State Home rate for domiciliary care. Payment for a veteran in a service center will not exceed eight hours in any day. Details may be found at **www.va.gov/HOMELESS/GPD.asp**.

CHALENG

The Community Homelessness Assessment, Local Education, and Networking Groups (CHALENG) for veterans is a nationwide initiative in which VA medical center and regional office directors work with other federal, state, and local agencies and nonprofit organizations to assess the needs of homeless veterans, develop action plans to meet identified needs, and develop directories that contain local community resources to be used by homeless veterans.

The guiding principle behind Project CHALENG is that no single agency can provide the full spectrum of services required to help homeless veterans become productive members of society. More than 10,000 representatives from non-VA organizations have participated in Project CHALENG initiatives, which include holding conferences at VA medical centers to raise awareness of the needs of homeless veterans, creating new partnerships in the fight against homelessness, and developing new strategies for future action.

The specific legislative requirements relating to Project CHALENG are that local medical center and regional office directors:

- Assess the needs of homeless veterans living in the area
- Make the assessment in coordination with representatives from state and local governments, appropriate federal departments and agencies and non-governmental community organizations that serve the homeless population

- Identify the needs of homeless veterans with a focus on health care, education and training, employment, shelter, counseling, and outreach
- Assess the extent to which homeless veterans' needs are being met
- Develop a list of all homeless services in the local area
- Encourage the development of coordinated services
- Take action to meet the needs of homeless veterans
- Inform homeless veterans of non-VA resources that are available in the community to meet their needs

At the local level, VA medical centers and regional offices designate CHALENG Points of Contact (POCs) who are responsible for the above requirements. These CHALENG POCs — usually local VA homeless center/project coordinators — work with local agencies throughout the year to coordinate services for homeless veterans. Details about this program may be found at **www.va.gov/homeless/chaleng.asp**.

The National Coalition for Homeless Veterans (NCHV)

The National Coalition for Homeless Veterans (NCHV), a 501(c)(3) non-profit organization governed by a 13-member board of directors, is the resource and technical assistance center for a national network of community-based service providers and local, state and federal agencies that provide emergency and supportive housing, food, health services, job training and placement assistance, legal aid, and case management support for hundreds of thousands of homeless veterans each year.

NCHV also serves as the primary liaison between the nation's care providers, Congress, and the executive branch agencies charged with helping them succeed in their work. NCHV's advocacy has strengthened and increased funding for virtually every federal homeless veteran assistance program in existence today.

Under a technical assistance grant awarded by the VA, NCHV provides guidance and information about program development, administration, governance, and funding to all of the nation's homeless veteran service providers.

Chapter 14

Burial, Funeral, and Memorial Benefits

A s a military veteran, you are entitled to burial, funeral, memorial, and other benefits to honor you for your significant contributions in service of the United States. This chapter will provide you with the full breakdown of benefits and entitlements. Spouses, surviving family members, and beneficiaries of veterans also should refer to this chapter. In fact, this chapter and the next chapter address the dependents of a veteran because they will be the ones who most likely will have to organize and apply for many of the benefits on behalf of the veteran.

Burial Benefits

The most basic of needs as soon as you have a loved one pass away is to figure out where, when, and with what money he or she is going to be buried. Fortunately, the VA has several burial options that veterans can set up before they pass away or that their families can set up for them after the fact.

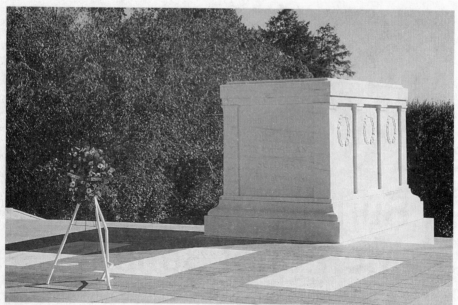

Tomb of the Unknown Solider at Arlington Cemetery

National cemetery

Burial benefits available include a grave site in any of the national cemeteries with available space, opening and closing of the grave, perpetual care, a Government headstone or marker, a burial flag, and a Presidential Memorial Certificate at no cost to the family. *Presidential Memorial Certificates will be discussed later in this chapter.* Cremated remains are buried or inurned in national cemeteries in the same manner and with the same honors as casketed

Arlington National Cemetery in Virginia

remains. Detailed instructions and information is available at **www.cem. va.gov/bbene_burial.asp.**

The Department of Veterans Affairs' (VA) National Cemetery Administration maintains 131 national cemeteries in 39 states (and Puerto Rico) and 33 soldiers' lots and monument sites. There is not a VA national cemetery in every state. A complete listing of all national cemeteries is available online at **www.cem.va.gov/cem/cems/listcem.asp**. State veterans cemeteries are available at **www.cem.va.gov/cem/grants/cemetery_list.asp**.

Burial benefits available for spouses and dependents buried in a national cemetery include burial with the veteran, perpetual care, and the spouse or dependent's name and date of birth and death will be inscribed on the veteran's headstone at no cost to the family.

Eligibility for Interment at Arlington National Cemetery

Eligibility for interment at Arlington National Cemetery is verified at the time of death and cannot be verified by the cemetery or accommodated before that time. The following individuals are eligible:

- Any active duty member of the Armed Forces (except those members serving on active duty for training only).

- Any retired member of the Armed Forces. If, at the time of death, a retired member of the Armed Forces is not entitled to receive retired pay stemming from his service in the Armed Forces until some future date, the retired member will not be eligible for ground burial.

- Any former member of the Armed Forces separated for physical disability before October 1, 1949, who served on active duty (other than for training) and who would have been eligible for retirement.

- Any former member of the Armed Forces whose last active duty (other than for training) military service terminated honorably and who has been awarded one of the following decorations:

o   Medal of Honor

o   Distinguished Service Cross (Air Force Cross or Navy Cross)

o   Distinguished Service Medal

o   Silver Star

o   Purple Heart

· An elective office of the United States Government
· Office of the chief justice of the United States or of an associate justice of the Supreme Court of the United States
· Any former prisoner of war who, while a prisoner of war, served honorably in the active military, naval, or air service, whose last period of active military, naval, or air service terminated honorably and who died on or after November 30, 1993.

Private cemetery

Burial benefits available for veterans buried in a private cemetery include a government headstone or marker, a burial flag, and a Presidential Memorial Certificate at no cost to the family. Some veterans also may be eligible for burial allowances as outlined below that cover the costs associated with the funeral and actual burial. Benefits are not available to spouses and dependents buried in a private cemetery.

Burial allowances

VA burial allowances are partial reimbursements of an eligible veteran's burial and funeral costs. VA will pay up to $2,000 toward burial expenses for service-related deaths. If the veteran is buried in a VA national cemetery, some or all of the cost of transporting the deceased may be reimbursed.

VA will pay up to $300 toward burial and funeral expenses for non-service-related deaths and a $300 plot-interment allowance. If the death happened while the veteran was in a VA hospital or under VA-contracted nursing home care, some or all of the costs for transporting the deceased's remains may be reimbursed. When the cause of death is not service-related, reimbursements generally are described as two payments: (1) a burial and funeral expense allowance, and (2) a plot interment allowance.

You may be eligible for a VA burial allowance if:

- You paid for a veteran's burial or funeral
- You have not been reimbursed by another government agency or some other source, such as the deceased veteran's employer
- The veteran was discharged under conditions other than dishonorable

In addition, at least one of the following conditions must be met:

- The veteran died because of a service-related disability.
- The veteran was receiving VA pension or compensation at the time of death.
- The veteran was entitled to receive VA pension or compensation but decided not to reduce his/her military retirement or disability pay.
- The veteran died in a VA hospital, in a nursing home under VA contract, or while in an approved state nursing home.

You can apply by filling out VA Form 21-530, Application for Burial Benefits. You should attach proof of the veteran's military service (DD 214), a death certificate, and copies of funeral and burial bills you have paid.

Headstones and Markers

The Department of Veterans Affairs (VA) furnishes upon request, at no charge to the applicant, a government headstone or marker for the grave of any deceased eligible veteran in any cemetery around the world.

Spouses and dependents buried in a private cemetery are not eligible for a government-provided headstone or marker.

Flat markers in granite, marble, and bronze and upright headstones in granite and marble are available. The style chosen must be consistent with existing monuments at the place of burial. Niche markers also are available to mark columbaria used for inurnment of cremated remains.

When burial or memorialization is in a national, post, or state veterans' cemetery, cemetery officials will order a headstone or marker based on inscription information provided by the next of kin.

Eligibility

Persons eligible for a government headstone or marker in a private cemetery are:

    a. Veterans and members of the Armed Forces (Army, Navy, Air Force, Marine Corps, Coast Guard)

        (1) Any member of the Armed Forces of the United States who dies on active duty

        (2) Any veteran who was discharged under conditions other than dishonorable

    b. Members of Reserve Components and Reserve Officers' Training Corps

(1) Reservists and National Guard members who, at time of death, were entitled to retired pay or would have been entitled but for being under the age of 60.

(2) Members of reserve components who die while hospitalized or undergoing treatment at the expense of the United States for injury or disease contracted or incurred under honorable conditions while performing active duty for training, inactive duty training, or undergoing such hospitalization or treatment.

(3) Members of the Reserve Officers' Training Corps of the Army, Navy, or Air Force who die under honorable conditions while attending an authorized training camp or on an authorized cruise, while performing authorized travel to or from that camp or cruise, or while hospitalized or undergoing treatment at the expense of the United States for injury or disease contracted or incurred under honorable conditions while engaged in one of those activities.

(4) Members of reserve components who, during a period of active duty for training, were disabled or died from a disease or injury incurred or aggravated in line of duty or, during a period of inactive duty training, were disabled or died from an injury incurred or aggravated in line of duty.

c. Commissioned officers, National Oceanic and Atmospheric Administration

(1) A commissioned officer of the National Oceanic and Atmospheric Administration with full-time duty on or after July 29, 1945

(2) A commissioned officer who served before July 29, 1945

(a) Was assigned to an area of immediate military hazard while in time of war, or of a presidentially declared national emergency as determined by the secretary of defense

(b) Served in the Philippine Islands on December 7, 1941, and continuously in such islands thereafter

      (c) Transferred to the Department of the Army or the Department of the Navy under the provisions of the Act of May 22, 1917

  d. Public Health Service

      (1) A commissioned officer of the Regular or Reserve Corps of the Public Health Service who served on full-time duty on or after July 29, 1945. If the service of the particular Public Health Service officer falls within the meaning of active duty for training, he or she must have been disabled or died from a disease or injury incurred or aggravated in the line of duty.

      (2) A commissioned officer of the Regular or Reserve Corps of the Public Health Service who performed full-time duty before July 29, 1945

         (a) In time of war

         (b) On detail for duty with the Army, Navy, Air Force, Marine Corps, or Coast Guard

         (c) While the service was part of the military forces of the United States pursuant to executive order of the president

      (3) A commissioned officer serving on inactive duty training whose death resulted from an injury incurred or aggravated in the line of duty

  e. World War II merchant mariners

      (1) United States merchant mariners with oceangoing service during the period of armed conflict, December 7, 1941, to December 31, 1946

      (2) United States merchant mariners who served on blockships in support of Operation Mulberry during World War II

Persons not eligible

You or your family member might not be eligible for a government-issued headstone if he or she falls under one of the following categories:

  a. Disqualifying characters of discharge: a person whose only separation from the Armed Forces was under dishonorable conditions or whose character of service results in a bar to veterans benefits

b. Discharge from draft: a person who was ordered to report to an induction station but was not inducted into military service

c. Person found guilty of a capital crime: Eligibility for a headstone or marker is prohibited if a person is convicted of a federal capital crime and sentenced to death or life imprisonment or is convicted of a state capital crime and sentenced to death or life imprisonment without parole. Federal officials are authorized to deny requests for headstones or markers to persons who are shown by clear and convincing evidence to have committed a federal or state capital crime but were not convicted of such crime because of flight to avoid prosecution or by death before trial.

d. Subversive activities: Any person convicted of subversive activities after September 1, 1959, shall have no right to burial in a national cemetery from and after the date of commission of such offense, based on periods of active military service commencing before the date of the commission of such offense, nor shall another person be entitled to burial on account of such an individual. Eligibility will be reinstated if the president of the United States grants a pardon.

e. Active or inactive duty for training: a person whose only service is active duty for training or inactive duty training in the National Guard or Reserve Component, unless the individual meets the following criteria:

(1) Reservists and National Guard members who, at time of death, were entitled to retired pay or would have been entitled, but for being under the age of 60

(2) Members of reserve components who die while hospitalized or undergoing treatment at the expense of the United States for injury or disease contracted or incurred under honorable conditions while performing active duty for training or inactive duty training, or undergoing such hospitalization or treatment

(3) Members of the Reserve Officers' Training Corps of the Army, Navy, or Air Force who die under honorable conditions while attending an authorized training camp or on an authorized cruise, while performing authorized travel to or from that camp or cruise, or while hospitalized or undergoing treatment at the expense of the United States for injury or disease contracted or incurred under honorable conditions while engaged in one of those activities

(4) Members of reserve components who, during a period of active duty for training, were disabled or died from a disease or injury incurred or aggravated in line of duty or, during a period of inactive duty training, were disabled or died from an injury incurred or aggravated in line of duty

    f. Other Groups: members of groups whose service has been determined not warranting entitlement to benefits administered by the secretary of veterans affairs

Setting government headstones and markers

Cemetery staff in national, military-post, and military-base cemeteries are responsible for setting the headstone or marker at no cost to the applicant. Some state veterans' cemeteries may charge the applicant a nominal fee for setting a government-furnished headstone or marker.

Arrangements for setting a government-furnished headstone or marker in a private cemetery are the applicant's responsibility, and all placement costs are at private expense.

Replacement headstones and markers

Headstones and markers previously furnished by the government may be replaced at government expense if badly deteriorated, illegible, stolen, or vandalized. They also may replace the headstone or marker if the inscription is incorrect, if it was damaged during shipping, or if the material or workmanship does not meet contract specifications.

If cemetery personnel damage a government headstone or marker in a private cemetery, the cemetery should pay all replacement costs.

Marble and granite headstones or markers that are permanently removed from a grave must be destroyed. Bronze markers must be returned to the contractor.

For guidance on obtaining a replacement headstone or marker, you may call the Memorial Programs Service Applicant Assistance Unit at 800-697-6947.

Burial Flags

A United States flag is provided, at no cost, to drape the casket or accompany the urn of a deceased veteran who served honorably in the U. S. Armed Forces. It is furnished to honor the memory of a veteran's military service to his or her country. The VA will furnish a burial flag for commemoration for each other than dishonorable discharged:

- Veteran who served during wartime
- Veteran who died on active duty after May 27, 1941
- Veteran who served after January 31, 1955
- Peacetime veteran who was discharged or released before June 27, 1950
- Certain persons who served in the organized military forces of the Commonwealth of the Philippines while in service of the U.S. Armed Forces and who died on or after April 25, 1951
- Certain former members of the Selected Reserves

The flag is given to the next-of-kin, as a keepsake, after its use during the funeral service. When there is no next-of-kin, VA will furnish the flag to a friend who is making a request for it. For those VA national cemeteries with an Avenue of Flags, families of veterans buried in these national cemeteries may donate the burial flags of their loved ones to be flown on patriotic holidays.

You may apply for the flag by completing VA Form 21-2008, Application for United States Flag for Burial Purposes. You may get a flag at any VA regional office or U.S. Post Office. The funeral director will help you obtain the flag. The law allows one flag for a veteran's funeral. It cannot be replaced it if it is lost, destroyed, or stolen. However, some veterans' organizations or other community groups may be able to help you get another flag.

The proper way to display the flag depends upon whether the casket is open or closed. VA Form 21-2008 (**www.vba.va.gov/pubs/forms/VBA-21-2008-ARE.pdf**) provides the correct method for displaying and folding the flag. The burial flag is not suitable for outside display because of its size and fabric. It is made of cotton and easily can be damaged by weather. You also can use this guide for proper folding of the flag: **www.va.gov/opa/publications/celebrate/flagfold.pdf**.

Presidential Memorial Certificates

A Presidential Memorial Certificate (PMC) is an engraved paper certificate, signed by the current president, to honor the memory of honorably discharged deceased veterans. This program was initiated in March 1962 by President John F. Kennedy and has been continued by all subsequent presidents.

The VA administers the PMC program by preparing the certificates, which bear the current president's signature expressing the country's grateful recognition of the veteran's service in the United States Armed Forces. Eligible recipients include the next of kin and loved ones of honorably discharged deceased veterans. More than one certificate may be provided.

Eligible recipients, or someone acting on their behalf, may apply for a PMC in person at any VA regional office or by U.S. mail or toll-free fax. Requests cannot be sent via email. Please be sure to enclose a copy of the veteran's discharge and death certificate to verify eligibility, along with VA Form 40-0247, Application for Presidential Memorial Certificate (**www.va.gov/vaforms/va/pdf/VA40-0247.pdf**).

Military Funeral Honors

Upon the family's request, Public Law 106-65 requires that every eligible veteran receive a military funeral honors ceremony, to include folding and presenting the United States burial flag and the playing of taps. The following groups are eligible for Military Funeral Honors:

- Military members on active duty or in the Selected Reserve

- Former military members who served on active duty and departed under conditions other than dishonorable

- Former military members who completed at least one term of enlistment or period of initial obligated service in the Selected Reserve and departed under conditions other than dishonorable

- Former military members discharged from the Selected Reserve due to a disability incurred or aggravated in the line of duty

The law defines a military funeral honors detail as consisting of two or more uniformed military persons, with at least one being a member of the veteran's parent service of the armed forces. The DOD program calls for funeral home directors to request military funeral honors on behalf of the veterans' family. However, the VA National Cemetery Administration cemetery staff also can assist with arranging military funeral honors at VA national cemeteries. Veteran organizations may assist in providing military funeral honors. When military funeral honors at a national cemetery are desired, they are arranged before the committal service by the funeral home.

Questions or comments concerning the DOD military funeral honors program may be answered on the website located at **www.militaryfuneralhonors.osd.mil**. To arrange military funeral honors, contact your local funeral home.

State Cemetery Grants Program

The Department of Veterans Affairs (VA) State Cemetery Grants Program assists states in providing grave sites for veterans in those areas where VA's national cemeteries cannot fully satisfy their burial needs.

Grants may be used only for the purpose of establishing, expanding, or improving veterans' cemeteries that are owned and operated by a state or U.S. territory. Aid can be granted only to states or U.S. territories. VA cannot provide grants to private organizations, counties, cities, or other government agencies.

VA now can provide up to 100 percent of the development cost for an approved project. For establishment of new cemeteries, VA can provide operating equipment. VA does not provide for acquisition of land. The value of the land cannot be considered an "allowable cost" under the grant. States are solely responsible for acquisition of the necessary land. Any state ceasing to own or operate a cemetery established, expanded, or improved using grant funds or using the funds for any other purpose than for which the grant was made will be liable for the total refund of all grants made for that cemetery. Federal funds also can be suspended or withdrawn for non-compliance with the terms and conditions of the grant.

Cemeteries established under the grant program must conform to the standards and guidelines pertaining to site selection, planning, and construction prescribed by VA. Cemeteries must be operated solely for the burial of service members who die on active duty, veterans, and their eligible spouses and dependent children. Any cemetery assisted by a VA grant must be maintained and operated according to the operational standards and measures of the National Cemetery Administration.

The administration, operation, and maintenance of a VA-supported state cemetery are solely the responsibility of the state. The secretary of veterans affairs is authorized to pay a plot or interment allowance (not to exceed $300) to a state for expenses incurred by the state in the burial of eligible veterans in a cemetery owned and operated by the state if the burial is performed at no cost to the veteran's next-of-kin.

VA's State Cemetery Grant Program is designed to complement VA's 131 national cemeteries across the country. This state cemetery grant program helps states establish new state veterans cemeteries and expand or improve existing state cemeteries. To date, the VA program has helped establish, expand, or improve 84 state veterans cemeteries in 41 states, Northern Mariana Islands and Guam, which provided more than 22,000 burials in fiscal year 2007. Since the program began in 1980, VA has awarded 162 grants totaling more than $312 million.

Chapter 15

Benefits for Surviving Spouses and Families of Veterans

s important as veterans' benefits are to the veteran, they can be equally as important to the veteran's family. Veterans entering a combat zone want to know that their surviving spouses, children, and families are going to be taken care of in their absence, be it temporary or permanent. If you are the surviving spouse or family of a military service member, you have certain benefits and entitlements because of your spouse or family member's military service. In addition to the health care benefits, educational assistance, and burial assistance that have been covered in previous chapters, survivors also are eligible for monetary benefits and financial assistance. This chapter will address survivors and dependents directly.

One of the more difficult tasks a survivor faces after the death of the veteran is completing the numerous claims forms for VA survivors' benefits.

The anxiety and fear of the unknown — who to call, what to do, or where to go for help — can be an unpleasant experience. For more information or to answer any questions this book did not cover, visit the VA survivor benefits website at **www.vba.va.gov/bln/dependents/index.htm**.

Documents needed when applying for survivor benefits:

- The veteran's discharge certificate or DD 214
- The veteran's VA claim's number or Social Security number
- The veteran's death certificate
- Government life insurance policy
- A copy of all marriage certificates and divorce decrees (if any)
- A copy of each child's birth certificate (or adoption order)
- Veteran's birth certificate to determine parents' benefits

Department of Defense Survivors Guide

One of the finest publications for survivors of service members who died on active duty is the Department of Defense Survivor's Guide to Benefits. You can download it at **www.militaryhomefront.dod.mil/dav/lsn/LSN/BINARY_RE-SOURCE/BINARY_CONTENT/1936651.pdf.**

Survivors of Service Members Who Die on Active Duty

Having your loved one die on active duty can be a painful and confusing time. Trying to make decisions for your deceased loved one as well as trying to address your concerns for the future can be overwhelming. To help you navigate through your benefits and entitlements, your military service will assign you a casualty assistance officer who will assist you with immediate needs and funeral arrangements and ensure you receive the benefits and privileges to which you are entitled and deserve.

Death gratuity

The death gratuity is a lump sum payment made by the DOD to the survivors of a service member who dies on active duty, active duty for training, inactive duty for training or within 120 days after release from active duty if the death is due to a service-related disability. The purpose of this payment is to assist survivors in meeting immediate living expenses. By law, only certain people are eligible to receive death gratuity payments and an order of precedence has been established as follows:

- Surviving spouse
- Children (in equal shares without regard to age or martial status if there is no surviving spouse)
- Parents, people acting as parents, brothers or sisters (if designated by the service member)

The death gratuity normally will be paid within 72 hours to the eligible beneficiary. Depending upon your service, you may elect to receive the money via electronic fund transfer or by check. If you choose check, your casualty assistance officer will deliver it. If the eligible beneficiary(ies) is a minor, payment may be delayed until guardianship is established. Questions about the payment of the death gratuity should be addressed to your casualty assistance officer.

Reimbursement of pay and allowances

Any pay or allowances due to the service member at the time of death will be paid to a designated beneficiary or a legal representative. Normally, pay and allowances due to the deceased service member will be limited to money earned during the month of death or since the last payday. Service members have the right to name any person as beneficiary for money remaining due at the time of death. The Defense Finance and Accounting Center will automatically forward necessary claim forms to the beneficiaries.

Dependency and Indemnity Compensation (DIC)

This compensation probably will be the most important part of your long-range financial planning. It is paid to eligible survivors of active duty service members and survivors of those veterans whose death is determined by the DVA to be service-related. It is a flat monthly payment, independent of the pay grade of the veteran. Use the following website to determine current payable rates: **www.vba.va.gov/bln/21/rates/comp0302.htm**. This payment is adjusted annually for cost of living increases and is nontaxable.

It is important to remember that DIC benefits will not be paid unless you apply for them. Your casualty assistance officer can arrange for you to meet with the local DVA office to file your application. Certain documents must be submitted with the application:

- Completed VA Form 21-534a
- DD Form 1300, Report of Casualty

This benefit is payable for the life of the spouse, provided the spouse does not remarry before the age of 57. However, should the remarriage end, DIC benefits can be reinstated. Income from other sources does not affect eligibility. The only requirements are proof of a relationship to the deceased service member and that the service member's death was service connected.

For more information contact your local DVA office, access the DVA website at **www.va.gov** or call 800-827-1000.

Vet Center Bereavement Counseling

Bereavement counseling now is being offered to parents, spouses, and children of Armed Forces personnel who died in the service of their country. Also eligible are family members of reservists and National Guardsmen who died while on duty. VA's bereavement counseling is provided at community-based Vet Centers located near the families. There is no cost for VA bereavement counseling.

Services are obtained by contacting Readjustment Counseling Service at 202-461-6530 or via electronic mail at **vetcenter.bereavementva.gov**, both of which are specific to this specialized service. RCS staff will assist families in contacting the nearest Vet Center. Often counseling can be made available in the family's home or where the family feels most comfortable.

The Survivor Benefit Plan

Retired pay stops when the veteran dies. The Survivor Benefit Plan (SBP) helps make up for the loss of part of this income. It pays eligible survivors an inflation-adjusted monthly income.

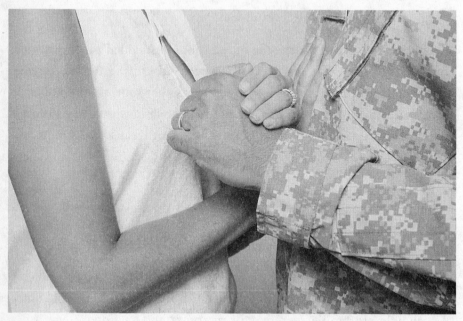

Regardless of whether your veteran family member died while on active duty or was retired from the military, survivors are entitled to Survivor Benefit Plan (SBP) payments. The SBP is not "insurance" that pays you a dividend payout upon the death of the service member. Instead, it is a program designed to continue partial retirement pay after the retired service member's death. The SBP annuity is determined by the base amount elected. The base amount may range from a minimum of $300 up to a maximum of full retired pay. The annuity is 55 percent of the base amount. Also, the base amount and the payments to the surviving spouse generally will increase at the same time and by the same percentage that cost-of-living adjustments (COLAs) are made to retired pay.

The veteran must pay premiums for SBP coverage once retired. Eligible children also may be SBP beneficiaries, either alone or added to spouse coverage. In the latter case, the children get benefits only if the spouse dies or remarries before age 55. Eligible children equally divide a benefit equal to 55 percent of the retired pay. Child coverage is relatively inexpensive because children get benefits only while they are still dependents.

SBP alone is not a complete estate plan. Other insurance and investments are important in meeting needs outside the scope of SBP. For example, SBP does not have a lump sum benefit that some survivors may need to meet immediate expenses upon a member's death.

The following table shows the costs associated with several "base amount" options and the benefits your spouse will receive based on these options.

Base Amount	SBP Costs *	SBP Benefits Before Age 62 (55% of Base Amount)
$300	$7.50	$165
$635	$15.87	$300
$800	$32.37	$440
$1,361	$88.46	$600
$1,400	$91.00	$770
$1,800	$117.00	$990
$2,200	$143.00	$1,210

* The SBP costs used in column two are calculated using the formula that provides the least cost. If the base amount was greater than or equal to $1,091, the formula in column one was used. For base amounts less than $1,091, the formula in column two was used.

The next table shows what can happen after retirement when inflation is a modest 4 percent per year. Retired pay is increased annually to keep pace with inflation. Survivor payments generally are increased at the same time, by the same percentage. These increases are made even after the member dies.

Your Age	Spouse's Age	Retired Pay	Cost of SBP	Benefit *
40	38	$1,000	$65.00	$550
45	43	$1,214	$78.91	$667

Your Age	Spouse's Age	Retired Pay	Cost of SBP	Benefit *
50	48	$1,474	$95.81	$810
55	53	$1,790	$116.35	$984
60	58	$2,175	$141.38	$1,196
65	63	$2,644	$171.86	$1,454
70	68	$3,213	$208.85	$1,767
80	78	$4,749	$308.69	$2,611
90	88	$7,024	$456.56	$3,863

In this example, the annuity at age 90 would be nearly four times the covered retired pay at age 40. This demonstrates two favorable features of SBP:

a. Payments can never run out.

b. Payments keep increasing along with the increased cost-of-living.

If you die shortly after retirement, your surviving spouse could receive cost-of-living adjusted payments for 50 years or more. Lifetime payments from an original election to cover $1,000 of retired pay could total more than one million dollars.

Tax savings

Monthly SBP costs are not included in your taxable federal income. The true cost for SBP is less than the amount deducted from retired pay because less federal tax will be paid. This also applies to most state income taxes. SBP payments to survivors are taxable, but spouses usually receive benefits when their total income is less and the extra tax exemption for being over age 65 is applicable. The surviving spouse's tax rate should be lower, and a long-run significant tax savings should result.

Former spouse coverage

SBP allows selection of coverage for former spouses. Costs and benefits under this option are identical to those for spouse coverage. Election of coverage for a former spouse precludes coverage of the current spouse and/or children of the current spouse.

When former spouse coverage is elected, the current spouse must be informed. Only one SBP election may be made. If there is more than one former spouse, the member must specify which one will be covered.

When electing the former spouse option, a member must give the finance center a written statement signed by both the member and the former spouse. It must state:

- Whether the election is made in order to comply with a court order

- Whether the election is made to comply with a voluntary written agreement related to a divorce action, and if so, whether that voluntary agreement is part of a court order for divorce, dissolution, or annulment

Child coverage

SBP was designed to give income protection not only to spouses, but also to children until they become self-supporting (i.e., until they are no longer dependents). Child coverage may be elected with or without spouse (former spouse) coverage.

Children are eligible for SBP payments as long as they are unmarried, under age 18, or under age 22 if still in school. A child who is disabled and incapable of self-support remains eligible if the disability occurred before age 18 (or before age 22 if a full-time student). Marriage at any age will terminate a child's eligibility. If former spouse and children coverage was elected, only those eligible children from the former marriage are covered.

Children who are under age 22 and pursuing a full-time course of study or training in a high school, trade school, technical or vocational institute, junior college, college, university, or comparable recognized educational institute are eligible to receive SBP benefits. While pursuing a full time course of study or training, a child whose 22nd birthday occurs before July 1 or after August 31 of a calendar year is considered age 22 on the first day of July after that birthday.

264 The Complete Guide to Veterans' Benefits

The payments for children equal 55 percent of the covered retired pay. All eligible children divide this benefit in equal shares. If the SBP election was for spouse (or former spouse) and children, the children receive payments only when the spouse (or former spouse) loses eligibility because of death or remarriage before age 55. The following is an example of benefit payments for four children and for the remaining children when one child becomes ineligible:

The example is based on the following information:

- Number of children: 4
- Base amount of retired pay: $2,000
- Base amount $2,000
- Base amount multiplied by 55 percent $1,100
- Amount of annuity divided by the number of children $1,100 / 4
- Amount each child will receive $275

If the oldest child becomes ineligible because of age, marriage or because he or she is no longer a full time student after the age of 18, only three children will receive payment and the annuity amount per child will be as follows:

- Annuity amount: $1,100
- Amount of annuity divided by the number of children $1,100 / 3
- Amount each child will receive $366.66

Social Security Administration Benefits

When a person who has worked and paid Social Security taxes dies, certain members of the family may be eligible for survivors benefits. Up to ten years of work is needed to be eligible for benefits, depending on the person's age at the time of death.

Social Security benefits can be paid to:

- A widow or widower — full benefits at full retirement age or reduced benefits as early as age 60

- A disabled widow or widower as early as age 50
- A widow or widower at any age if he or she takes care of the deceased's child who is under age 16 or disabled and receiving Social Security benefits
- Unmarried children under 18, or up to age 19 if they are attending high school full time. Under certain circumstances, benefits can be paid to stepchildren, grandchildren, or adopted children
- Children at any age who were disabled before age 22 and remain disabled
- Dependent parents age 62 or older

SSA Calculators can help you figure how much your benefits will be: **www.ssa.gov/planners/calculators.htm**.

How work affects survivors' benefits

You can receive Social Security benefits and work at the same time. However, depending on your age, your benefits could be reduced if you earn more than certain amounts as outlined at **http://ssa.gov/pubs/10069.html#howmuch**.

How divorce affects survivors' benefits

If your divorced spouse dies, you can receive benefits as a widow/widower if the marriage lasted ten years or longer and you are age 60 or older (or age 50 if you are disabled.) Benefits paid to a surviving divorced spouse who is 60 or older (age 50 if disabled) will not affect the benefit rates for other survivors receiving benefits.

How remarriage affects survivors' benefits

You cannot receive survivor's benefits if you remarry before the age of 60 unless the latter marriage ends, whether by death, divorce, or annulment. If you remarry after age 60 (50 if disabled), you still can collect benefits on your former spouse's record. When you reach age 62 or older, you may get retirement benefits on the record of your new spouse if they are higher.

Your remarriage would have no effect on the benefits being paid to your children.

How retirement affects survivors' benefits

If you are collecting survivor's benefits, you can switch to your own retirement benefits (assuming you are eligible and your retirement rate is higher than the widow/widower's rate) as early as age 62.

In many cases, you can begin receiving retirement benefits either on your own or your spouse's record at age 62 and then switch to the other benefit when you reach full retirement age, if that amount is higher.

Conclusion

As a 30-year veteran, I can tell you the transition from military life to civilian is a hard one. The transition from veteran to disabled veteran, combat-wounded veteran, or severely disabled is significantly more traumatic and life changing. Hundreds of programs and benefits can ease this transition and provide you with the financial, medical, and other support you may require.

It is my sincere hope that this book will be used as a valued reference guide to benefits for our military veterans and provide them with valuable answers surrounding entitlements and benefits. A few more good sources of information about what Congress is proposing for changes in benefits is the House Committee on Veterans Affairs, which is found at **http://veterans.house.gov/legislation/110legislation.shtml**, and the U.S. Senate Committee on Veterans Affairs, which is found at **http://veterans.senate.gov**.

I cannot stress enough the wealth of information on state veterans' websites. They are packed with information on benefits and have specific programs and entitlements for your specific state.

Best wishes to all of our U.S. military veterans, and a heartfelt thank you from the Brown Family for your selfless service and sacrifice to our great nation.

God Bless America!

Commander Bruce C. Brown
United States Coast Guard

Appendix

Veterans Administration Organizations

**Veterans Health Administration
(www.va.gov/health/default.asp)**
With 157 hospitals nationwide, VHA manages one of the largest health care systems in the United States. VAMCs (Veterans Administration Medical Centers) within a Veterans Integrated Service Network (VISN) work together to provide efficient, accessible health care to veterans in their areas. The VHA also conducts research and education, and provides emergency medical preparedness.

**Veterans Benefits Administration
(www.vba.va.gov/VBA)**
VBA provides benefits and services to the veteran population through 58 VA regional offices. Some of the benefits and services provided by VBA to veterans and their dependents include compensation and pension, education, loan guaranty, and insurance.

National Cemetery Administration
(www.cem.va.gov)

NCA is responsible for providing burial benefits to veterans and eligible dependents. The delivery of these benefits involves managing 131 national cemeteries nationwide, providing grave markers worldwide, administering the State Cemetery Grants Program that complements the National Cemeteries Network, and providing Presidential Memorial Certificates to next of kin of deceased veterans.

Board of Contract Appeals
(www2.va.gov/directory/guide/facility.asp?ID=2005)

The Department of Veterans Affairs Board of Contract Appeals considers and determines appeals from decisions of contracting officers pursuant to the Contract Disputes Act of 1978.

Board of Veterans' Appeals
(www.bva.va.gov)

The board reviews benefit claims determinations made by local VA offices and issues decision on appeals. The board members, attorneys experienced in veterans law and in reviewing benefit claims, are the only ones who can issue board decisions.

Center for Women Veterans
(www.va.gov/womenvet)

The mission of the Center for Women Veterans is to ensure women veterans have access to VA benefits and services, to ensure that VA health care and benefits programs are responsive to the gender-specific needs of women veterans, to perform outreach to improve women veterans awareness of VA services, benefits and eligibility, and to act as the primary adviser to the secretary for veterans affairs on all matters related to programs, issues, and initiatives for and affecting women veterans.

Office of Acquisition and Material Management (OAMM)
(www.va.gov/oal)

OAMM is responsible for overseeing the acquisition, storage, and distribution of supplies, services, and equipment used by VA facilities and other government agencies. OAMM manages pharmaceuticals, medical supplies and equipment, and nonperishable subsistence through its procurement system.

Office of Alternate Dispute Resolution (ADR) and Mediation
(**www.va.gov/adr**)
This office provides effective training and consulting in conflict resolution and ADR (emphasizing mediation) to VA organizations and employees.

Office of Budget
(**www.va.gov/budget**)
The Office of Budget is the focal point for the departmental budget formulation and execution, the Capital Investment Board and Performance Reporting.

Office of Public Affairs and Intergovernmental Affairs (OPAIA)
(**www.va.gov/opa**)
OPAIA has two major offices, Public Affairs and Intergovernmental Affairs. The primary mission of public affairs is to provide information to the nation's veterans and their eligible dependents and survivors through news media concerning available benefits and programs. Intergovernmental Affairs interacts with federal, state, and local government agencies and officials in developing and maintaining a positive and productive relationship.

Office of Congressional Affairs (OCA)
(**www.va.gov/oca**)
OCA is the principal point of contact between the department and Congress and is the oversight and coordinating body for the department's congressional relations. The office serves in an advisory capacity to the secretary and deputy secretary and other VA managers concerning policies, programs, and legislative matters in which congressional committees or individual members of Congress have expressed an interest.

Office of Employment Discrimination Complaint Adjudication (OEDCA)
(www.oedca.va.gov)

OEDCA maintains a high quality and high performing workforce and ensures fairness, integrity, and trust throughout the complaint adjudication phase of the equal employment opportunity complaint resolution process.

Office of Financial Management (OFM)
(www.ofm.wa.gov)

OFM continually improves the quality of the VA's financial services through the development of sound financial policies and the promotion of efficient financial management systems, operations, policies, and practices.

Office of the General Counsel (OGC)
(www.va.gov/ogc)

The OGC identifies and meets the legal needs of the VA.

Office of Human Resources and Administration (OHRA)
(www.va.gov/ofcadmin)

OHRA's functional areas include human-resources management, administrative policies and functions, equal opportunity policies and functions, and security and law enforcement.

Office of Information and Technology (OIT)
(www.oit.va.gov)

OIT activities include integrated business and information technology (IT) planning; security and contingency planning to protect information and privacy across VA systems and networks; reviews to evaluate the performance of IT programs; review and approval of IT acquisitions; facilitation of intra- and intergovernmental partnerships; educating and informing the Department of IT, initiatives and legislation; and sharing lessons learned.

Office of the Inspector General (OIG)
(www.va.gov/oig)

The OIG provides service to veterans, VA employees, and citizens concerned with good government.

Office of Occupational Safety and Health
(www.va.gov/vasafety)
The staff ensures that the VA complies with requirements of the federal, Occupational Safety and Health Administration (OSHA), Joint Commission for Accreditation of Healthcare Organizations (JCAHO), and VA standards.

Office of Policy, Planning and Preparedness (OPPP)
(www.va.gov/op3)
OPPP facilitates, coordinates, and validates the department's policy development and formulation processes; coordinates VA's strategic planning process and implementation of the Government Performance and Results Act requirements; supports the identification, development, analysis, and review of issues affecting veterans' programs; links and supplements the actuarial and quantitative analysis capabilities of VA in support of major policy inquiries; serves as VA's focal point for access to and availability of official data; coordinates the independent evaluation of VA program performance; and fosters quality management techniques and procedures throughout VA.

Office of Regulation Policy and Management (ORPM)
(www.va.gov/orpm)
The Office of Regulation Policy and Management (ORPM) is responsible for the centralized management, control, and coordination of all VA regulations. ORPM supervises the VA's Regulation Rewrite Project, a comprehensive effort to review, reorganize, and rewrite VA regulations lacking clarity, consistency, or logical organization. ORPM also is responsible for devising and implementing new procedures to centralize control and improve secretarial oversight, management, drafting efficiency, policy resolution, impact analysis, and coordination of diverse VA regulations.

Office of Small and Disadvantaged Business Utilization (OSDBU)
(www.va.gov/osdbu)
OSDBU advocates for the maximum practicable participation of small, small disadvantaged, veteran-owned, women-owned, and empowerment zone businesses in contracts awarded by the VA and in subcontracts, which are awarded by VA's prime contractors.

Suicide Prevention Lifeline

The National Suicide Prevention Lifeline has been enhanced to provide a new service for veterans in crisis. Call 800-273-TALK (8255) and press 1 to be connected immediately to VA suicide prevention and mental health service professionals.

State and Federal Veterans Facilities

Veterans' facilities offer a wealth of information, benefits, and services to which you may be entitled. You earned benefits from your service, and you are entitled to those benefits. Learn what is available in your local area, through the federal government and your state government, and take advantage of your benefits — you earned them.

Federal veterans facilities

VA makes it easy for you to find what is available in your local area. You can go to the following places to search for federal facilities:

- Veterans Health Administration: **www1.va.gov/directory/guide/division_flsh.asp?dnum=1**
- Veterans Benefits Administration: **www1.va.gov/directory/guide/division_flsh.asp?dnum=3**
- National Cemetery Administration: **www1.va.gov/directory/guide/division_flsh.asp?dnum=4**
- Vet Centers: **www2.va.gov/directory/guide/hq_flsh.asp?**
- VA Central Offices: **www1.va.gov/directory/guide/hq_flsh.asp?**
- Gravesite locator: **http://gravelocator.cem.va.gov/j2ee/servlet/NGL_v1**
- Facilities by state: **www1.va.gov/directory/guide/allstate_flsh.asp?**
- Facility listing: **www1.va.gov/directory/guide/rpt_fac_list.cfm**

Toll-free numbers for contacting VA

VA Benefits 800-827-1000

- Burial
- Civilian Health and Medical Program of the Department of Veterans Affairs (CHAMPVA)
- Death pension
- Dependency indemnity compensation
- Direct deposit
- Directions to VA Benefits Regional Offices
- Disability compensation
- Disability pension
- Education
- Home loan guaranty
- Life insurance
- Medical care
- Vocational rehabilitation and employment

Education (GI Bill) 888-442-4551

Health care benefits 877-222-8387

Income verification and means testing 800-929-8387

Life insurance 800-669-8477

Mammography helpline 888-492-7844

Special issues — Gulf War/Agent Orange/Project Shad/Mustard Agents and Lewisite/Ionizing Radiation 800-749-8387

Status of headstones and markers 800-697-6947

Telecommunications device for the deaf (TDD) 800-829-4833

For health care services, contact your nearest VA medical facility.

State veterans facilities

State veterans facilities are abundant and are surprisingly accessible to most areas in each state. The best way to find those in your local area is to contact your state veterans affairs division, visit your state VA website, or search the Internet for VA facilities in your area. You will be impressed with what the state has to offer our veterans.

Important phone numbers

Bereavement counseling 202-461-6530
Civilian Health and Medical Program (CHAMPVA) 800-733-8387
Education..888-442-4551
Federal Recovery Coordination program 877-732-4456
Foreign Medical Program 888-820-1756
Headstones and markers...800-697-6947
Health care..877-222-8387
Homeless veterans 877-424-3838
Home loans..888-244-6711
Life insurance..800-669-8477
National Cemetery Scheduling Office 800-535-1117
National Suicide Prevention Lifeline 800-273-8255
Pension Management Center...877-294-6380
Presidential Memorial Certificate program 202-565-4964
Special health issues...800-749-8387
Spina bifida/children of women Vietnam veterans..............888-820-1756
Telecommunication device for the deaf (TDD) 800-829-4833
VA benefits..800-827-1000
Women veterans..202-461-1070

Important websites

Burial and memorial benefits...**www.cem.va.gov**
CHAMPVA ....**www.va.gov/hac/forbeneficiaries/forbeneficiaries.asp**
Education benefits...**www.gibill.va.gov**
Federal jobs..**www.usajobs.gov**
Health care eligibility ....**www.va.gov/healtheligibility**
Home loan guaranty...**www.homeloans.va.gov**
Life insurance..**www.insurance.va.gov**
Memorial Certificate Program ....**www.cem.va.gov/pmc.asp**
Mental health ....**www.mentalhealth.va.gov**
My HealtheVet..**www.myhealth.va.gov**
National Resource Directory ....**www.nationalresourcedirectory.gov**
Prosthetics...**www.prosthetics.va.gov**

Record............................ **www.archives.gov/st-louis/military-personnel**

Returning service members.. **www.oefoif.va.gov**

Women veterans... **www.womenshealth.va.gov**

VA Vet Centers... **www.vetcenter.va.gov**

VA home page.. **www.va.gov**

VA benefit payment rates............................**www.vba.va.gov/bln/21/rates**

VA forms.................................**www.va.gov/vaforms/search_action.asp**

Veterans employment and training...............................**www.dol.gov/vets**

Nonprofit Veterans Organizations

Military service members and, in particular, military veterans and their families, enjoy an immense support base. There are dozens of outstanding veterans organizations whose entire purpose is to support veterans, perform veterans advocacy work, lobby for veterans benefits, and provide a wealth of information and support services. Although there are likely hundreds of such groups, some of the more popular are listed here for you.

You can easily find others by using Google or your favorite search engine. Additionally, all states have their own veterans' websites that list nonprofit organizations operating within your state.

American Ex-Prisoners of War 3201 East Pioneer Parkway, #40 Arlington, TX 76010 817-649-2979 **www.axpow.org**	American Legion P.O. Box 1055 Indianapolis, IN 46206 317-630-1200 **http://legion.org**
American Red Cross 2025 E. Street, NW Washington, DC 20006 800-733-2767 **www.redcross.org**	AMVETS 4647 Forbes Boulevard Lanham, MD 20706-4380 301-459-9600 301-459-7924 fax amvets@amvets.org **www.amvets.org**

Blinded Veterans Association 477 H Street, NW Washington, DC 20001-2694 202-371-8880 202-371-8258 fax bva@bva.org **www.bva.org**	Congressional Medal of Honor Society of the United States of America 40 Patriots Point Road Mt. Pleasant, SC 29464 843-884-8862 843-884-1471 fax **www.cmohs.org**
Disabled American Veterans P.O. Box 14301 Cincinnati, OH 45250-0301 859-441-7300 **www.dav.org**	Fleet Reserve Association 125 N. West Street Alexandria, VA 22314-2754 703-683-1400 adminfra@fra.org **www.fra.org**
Military Chaplains Association of the United States of America P.O. Box 7056 Arlington, VA 22207-7056 703-533-5890 703-533-5890 fax chaplains@mca.usa.org **http://mca-usa.org**	Military Order of the Purple Heart of the U.S.A., Inc. 5413-C Backlick Road Springfield, VA 22151 703-354-2140 info@purpleheart.org **www.purpleheart.org**
Military Order of the World Wars 435 North Lee Street Alexandria, VA 22314-2301 877-320-3774 **www.militaryorder.net**	National Amputation Foundation, Inc. 40 Church Street Malverne, NY 11565 516-887-3600 516-887-3667 fax **www.nationalamputation.org**
National Association for Black Veterans, Inc. P.O. Box 11432 Milwaukee, WI 53211-0432 800-842-4597 414-342-1073 fax info@nabvets.com **www.nabvets.com**	National Association of State Directors of Veterans Affairs (NASDVA) Bataan Memorial Bldg. 407 Galisteo St. Room 142 Santa Fe, NM 87504 866-433-8387 **www.nasdva.us**

Navy Club of the United States of America 6243 S. 150 W. Lafayette, IN 47909-8909 800-628-7265 enewman@tctc.com **www.navyclubusa.org**	Navy Mutual Aid Association 29 Carpenter Road Henderson Hall Arlington, VA 22212 800-628-6011 703-945-1441 fax **www.navymutual.org**
Non Commissioned Officers Association 9330 Corporate Drive, Suite 701 Selma, Texas 78154 800-662-2620 **www.ncoausa.org**	Paralyzed Veterans of America 801 18th Street, NW Washington, DC 20006 800-424-8200 info@pva.org **www.pva.org**
The Retired Enlisted Association 1111 S. Abilene Court Aurora, CO 80012-4909 800-338-9337 303-752-0835 fax treahq@trea.org **www.trea.org**	U.S. Submarine Veterans P.O. Box 3870 Silverdale, WA 98383-3870 360-337-2978 office@ussvi.org **www.ussvi.org**
Veterans Assistance Foundation, Inc. P.O. Box 109 Newburg, WI 53060 262-692-6333 262-692-6467 fax **http://vafvets.org**	Veterans of Foreign Wars of the United States 406 West 34th Street (Broadway at 34th Street) Kansas City, MO 64111 816-756-3390 202-543-6719 fax info@vfw.org **www.vfw.org**
Veterans of the Vietnam War, Inc./Vets. Coalition 805 South Township Boulevard Pittston, PA 18640-3327 570-603-9740 570-603-9741 fax **www.vvnw.org**	Vietnam Veterans of America 8719 Colesville Road, Suite 100 Silver Spring, MD 20910 800-882-1316 **www.vva.org**

Women's Army Corps Veterans Association P.O. Office Box 5577 Fort McClellan, AL 36205 256-820-6824 info@armywomen.org **www.armywomen.org**	

Other veterans' organizations that may not yet have congressional charter include:

National Veterans Organization (**www.nvo.org**)

American Gulf War Veterans Association (**www.gulfwarvets.com**)

Gulf War Veterans Resource (**www.gulfweb.org**)

Iraq and Afghanistan Veterans of America (**http://iava.org**)

Many other great organizations support veterans. This certainly is not intended to be an all-inclusive list, but it should serve as a good reference to start your research.

Resources

Budahn, P. J. *Veteran's Guide To Benefits (Veteran's Guide to Benefits)*, 4th Edition. Mechanicsburg, Pennsylvania: Stackpole Books, 2005.

Kaplan. *Kaplan Scholarships 2008: Billions of Dollars in Free Money for College (Kaplan Scholarships)*. New York: Kaplan Publishing, 2007.

Leyva, Meredith. *Married to the Military: A Survival Guide for Military Wives, Girlfriends, and Women in Uniform*. New York: Fireside, 2003.

Michel, Christopher P. and Norman Schwarzkopf. *The Military Advantage: A Comprehensive Guide to Your Military & Veterans Benefits*. New York, New York: Simon & Schuster, 2005.

Roche, John D. *The Veteran's Survival Guide: How to File and Collect on VA Claims, Second Edition*. Dulles, Virginia: Potomac Books, Inc., 2006.

U.S. Government. *Veterans Benefits Guide — Compensation, Appeals, Disability, Medical Care, Insurance Programs, Plans for Families, GI Bill, Home Loan Programs* (Two CD-ROM Set). Progressive Management, 2007.

Author Biography

Commander Bruce C. Brown has served in the Coast Guard for more than 30 years. He took command of Coast Guard Base Elizabeth City, NC in May 2014 following an assignment at Coast Guard Sector St. Petersburg where he served as Logistics Department Head and Commanding Officer of Military Personnel. He was directly responsible for all aspects of mission support for 5 Multi-Mission Small Boat Stations, Six Patrol Boats, Coastal Buoy Tender, Inland Construction Tender, Aids to Navigation Team, 32 Small Boats and four tenant commands supporting more than 2,700 Active Duty, Civilians, Reserve and Auxiliary Members.

Commander Bruce C. Brown
United States Coast Guard
Land O' Lakes, Florida • 2014

As Base Commanding Officer, he is responsible maintaining 800 acres of real estate, including runways and taxiways, roadways, buildings, 72 Coast Guard owned family housing units, a Servicing Personnel Office that maintains pay and personnel records for all local Coast Guard members, providing transportation and logistics support, and medical and dental services for thousands of Coast Guard active duty personnel, 500 dependents and military retirees in the area.

Commander Brown enlisted in the Coast Guard in 1984 and his first assignment was USCGC FIREBUSH in Kodiak, Alaska. Following graduation from Storekeeper "A" school he was stationed at Loran-C Station Malone, Group Fort Macon, USCGC STORIS and Aviation Technical Training Center. Aboard STORIS he served as independent duty Storekeeper and qualified as Boarding Officer in complex Bering Sea fisheries law enforcement as well as Maritime Law Enforcement Instructor and was recipient of the prestigious Douglas A. Munro Award for Inspirational Leadership as well as the American Society of Military Comptrollers Award of Excellence. Commander Brown is a 1995 graduate of Officer Candidate School and has served in a diverse series of operational and staff assignments including Officer in Charge Law Enforcement Detachment where he led deployments in support of embargo operations against the Former Republic of Yugoslavia as well as numerous counter-narcotic patrols in the Caribbean theater aboard United States Navy and British Royal Navy warships. He subsequently served in Financial Management and Comptroller positions at the Coast Guard Finance Center, Air Station Clearwater and Coast Guard Headquarters. Prior to serving at Sector St. Petersburg, Commander Brown was assigned as Deputy Chief of Resources for the Seventh District in Miami, Florida where he oversaw the administration of a $36 million operating budget supporting more than 10,000 personnel, as well as facilities planning and management of the third largest shore facility inventory & physical plant in the Coast Guard. During this tour he served as Finance Section Chief (FSC) for Operation UNIFIED RESPONSE and Operation SOUTH EAST WATCH - HAITI following a catastrophic magnitude 7.0 Earthquake centered near Port-au-Prince, Haiti which devastated the city and surrounding areas, resulting in more than 200,000 lives lost.

Commander Brown is an award-winning author of 14 books and two-time recipient of the Coast Guard Chief Financial Officers Award for Excellence. Commander Brown's military decorations include five Meritorious Service Medals, five Commendation Medals, two Achievement Medals, Armed Forces Service Medal, Armed Forces Expeditionary Medal, NATO Medal and many others. He earned a permanent Cutterman's Pin in 1996. Commander Brown is a native of Bayshore, New York and has been happily married for 30 years to the former Vonda R. Randall. They have three sons: Dalton, Jordan and Colton.

Index